Nataly von Eschstruth, Mary J. Safford

The opposite House

A Novel

Nataly von Eschstruth, Mary J. Safford

The opposite House
A Novel

ISBN/EAN: 9783337041342

Printed in Europe, USA, Canada, Australia, Japan

Cover: Foto ©ninafisch / pixelio.de

More available books at **www.hansebooks.com**

THE OPPOSITE HOUSE

A NOVEL

FROM THE GERMAN OF

NATALY VON ESCHSTRUTH

Author of "*A Priestess of Comedy,*" "*A Princess of the Stage,*" "*Her Little Highness,*" etc. . . . .

TRANSLATED BY

MARY J. SAFFORD

NEW YORK AND LONDON
STREET & SMITH, PUBLISHERS

Copyright, 1894
By Robert Bonner's Sons

(*All rights reserved*)

The Opposite House

THE OPPOSITE HOUSE.

CHAPTER I.

A NIGHT OF STORM.

DARKNESS had gathered in Frau Gertrude's old-fashioned chamber.

The rain pattered monotonously against the panes of the lofty window and trickled in heavy drops down to the sill. The flickering light of the street lamps cast an uncertain glimmer upon the ancient mansion, whose stone entrance-posts had seen numerous generations of the honored family of merchants pass in and out of the vaulted doorway. A few pedestrians still glided past in the darkness like dim, gray shadows, and from the distant main street echoed the dull rumble of swiftly moving vehicles.

Gertrude's eyes, glittering with the light of fever, were fixed steadily upon the dark oaken door; her restless gaze constantly wandered over the carved figures, counting the interwoven balls and flowers until they danced confusedly before her, and changed into all the strange shapes which the fantastic fingers of fever can paint.

"Not yet—not yet!" she moaned, turning her face, whose cheeks glowed with an ominous flush, upon the cool pillows. "Oh, God, why dost Thou inflict this pang upon my dying hour?"

She raised herself excitedly. The terrible cough again attacked her weak chest, making her gasp for air and breath. At last the paroxysm passed away.

"Go, Gretlis, go," she whispered faintly; and the old servant covered her tearful eyes with her hand, and pleaded:

"You ought not to be alone, Frau Gertrude. Let me stay until he comes!"

The sick woman laughed almost bitterly.

"Until he comes! But listen, Gretlis. Never desert him, whatever happens. Watch over him, guard him, be a second mother to my boy. And over yonder—you know, Gretlis, the house with the gray escutcheon—say nothing to him about it, but protect him and don't permit him to continue to hate. Now go—I am weary. Pray—pray for my child!"

Frau Gertrude held out her burning hand; then her fixed gaze followed the old woman's figure as she noiselessly vanished behind the dark door.

The old clock struck eleven dull strokes with a creaking, rattling sound. Just at that moment a carriage rolled along the street and stopped below; laughing voices called good-night to each other noisily; a loud knock sounded on the door of the house; hasty steps sprang up the stairs. Some one whispered outside with old Gretlis; then came a low exclamation of terror, followed by silence. The sick woman's eyes rested steadily upon the folds of the curtain, but her lips quivered and her fingers played restlessly with the fine linen sheets. The door opened softly, and Frau Gertrude's son entered the room.

The young man, who had a slender, powerful figure and a fine, intelligent face, came slowly forward. Gertrude did not stir.

"Mother!" he cried in a piercing tone. "Mother!"

A few steps brought him to her bedside, where, throwing himself on his knees, he buried his face in her cold hands. A strange tremor flitted around the dying woman's lips.

"Where were you, Traugott? Gambling? At the green table?"

A grave, mute glance met his. Then she slowly drew her hand from his clasp and turned her gray head toward the wall, bitter tears coursing down her grief-worn cheeks.

"Go!"

"Mother!" groaned Traugott. "Mother, forgive me!" And overwhelmed by terrible agitation, he threw his arms around her neck and sobbed like a child. "Let me hold and kiss your hand. Do not shrink from me, mother! By Heaven, I do not deserve it! Whatever I may have done, whatever sins I have committed, whatever follies have sprung from my recklessness, my heart is still untainted. I still possess a large fortune. I am rich, and, thank Heaven, I am also young. Oh, mother, I can work, and if hitherto I have neglected to do so, I will make amends doubly for the lost hours, the wasted years."

He again fell upon his knees at her side, and rested his head on her clasped hands.

Gertrude raised her dark eyes heavenward; her mute gaze wandered through the parted curtains to the sky, where the moon burst through the torn clouds, then she laid her trembling hands tenderly upon her son's head.

"May God help you, my boy! Be noble and upright, though I am no longer with you—can no longer guard you and urge you by my words to better paths ! Conquer that terrible passion whose demon leads to destruction, whose end is darkness and horror. God gave you a good heart, my son ; keep it pure and noble. Drop gambling, Traugott; it will bring you to ruin, and accursed be the man who does not hold his mother's last words sacred !"

Her tones grew fainter and more hurried, her gasping breath shorter, and when the pale moon emerged completely from behind the clouds a despairing son was kneeling beside the death-bed of the mother, whose last blessing was given to her wayward child.

* * * * * *

The next morning strange rumors were current in the ancient capital. Frau Gertrude Gerrald was dead. She had died, not suddenly, not slowly, but after years of wasting grief for her only son, yet it was an event discussed everywhere with equal interest.

The officers' *casino* was nearly empty. There were only two members of a cavalry regiment seated at a table.

" Have you heard that Frau Gerrald is dead?" asked Baron Linden, filling his companion's glass a second time. " Now a gay life may be expected.

The locks of the chests of money will no longer be watched. I suppose the son was again at the gaming-table yesterday? They say he did not arrive in time to see her alive. By the way, I expected to meet you yesterday at the Chênois's rooms; she had a reception."

"I? At the Chênois's?" yawned Horster.

"Yes, you. Rumor says that for some time you have paid homage to the noble art, and most dutifully attended Heloise's triumphal chariot. Some gossips also assert that the flower-dealers are making big profits from this fancy. Well, is the news true?"

The other quietly uncorked a second bottle and let the sparkling drops run slowly into his glass.

"Of course it's true," he said, with a careless smile. "It's really too bad for me to be obliged to confess it, but, *entre nous*, you understand me, Linden. Why shouldn't the fiery-eyed Circe bewitch me as well as everybody else—the many hundreds who have not half my advantages? The ballet, my friend, is in our day the court of first instance to which Ekkehard and Don Juan must alike pay toll. I almost marvel that above apple and cross a little gold slipper does not shine—a slipper composed of all the names which, by a few *entrechats*, have pitilessly forced crowned heads to their feet! Prinz Lothar is never absent from the Chênois's receptions, and, it is said, must have lavished thousands to press upon her brow a glittering coronal. The most absurd thing about the whole matter to me, however, is that his highness has so long had a rival in a simple miller—this 'Prince of the Mill,' as he is called. He remains at her feet like a foolish boy, bearing her numberless caprices with a patience worthy of a better cause. Yes, this Heloise is a witch, and if I, who am no fool, allow her to lead me about by the nose, what do I gain by it? Endless vexations! Never mind," he yawned, rising. "Will you go to the ring with me, Linden? Lieutenant von Hühn is going to ride his new bay."

"No; I have a visit to pay. I've already deferred it three weeks," replied Linden, slowly stroking his fair mustache. "I must hurry to reach Frau von Lienau's. Perhaps they will give me the cold shoulder; but aid me, Munchausen, to tell them such marvelous tales of the hero of the day that they will not have the least inclination to do so." Laughing gayly, he buckled on his sword and took his helmet under his arm: "*Au revoir!*"

CHAPTER II.

THE PRINCE OF THE MILL.

Young Gerrald had cared little for the gossip of the worthy citizens of D——, whether with noble indignation they condemned him or defended him against all the slanderous tongues. He had locked himself into the bow-window room to keep watch alone beside his mother's coffin.

No one except old Gretlis had seen him during this time. She had obstinately begged admission urgently to entreat her young master to eat, and now and then had asked him for counsel. Then Traugott himself helped her arrange a little room in the attic, where the old woman was henceforth to live and take charge of the empty house.

The black coffin had been lowered into the earth quietly, without display, and the young merchant now stood alone and desolate in the dead woman's chamber.

A very singular change had occurred in his whole nature, and was reflected in his pale features. The dark-blue eyes looked grave and earnest beneath their arched brows, the lips closed firmly over the white teeth, and a deep, almost melancholy line appeared on his brow. Traugott Gerrald had matured to manhood. Only a few days before his features had been characterless, boyish and yet *blasé*—a handsome profile, behind whose open brow there lived only an unbridled love of pleasure. And now had come the crisis when fate, for the first time, strips the smile from the lips, when with rude hand it cuts deep lines and imprints upon the face the sacred signet whose device is—" Experience."

A broad band of black *crepe* was wound around his arm. Before him still lay a fresh flower, which he had taken from his mother's coffin as a last memento.

He pressed it to his lips almost timidly; the white blossom seemed to him a sacred legacy.

"My talisman! My sacred relic!" He opened his elegant note-book to conceal it among the leaves. But all the pages were filled. Here lay a pomegranate-blossom. "From Heloise's curls!" was written beneath, and the beginning of a student's drinking song. No, that was no place for the white flower of death!

A deep flush mounted slowly to his pale brow. Here were figures; big, black figures, hastily scrawled—at the gaming-table!

With a passionate gesture, the young man flung down the book, and tearing out the leaves, burned them on the hearth. Then he placed the white flower in a gold box and hid it in his breast.

*   *   *   *   *   *

The unexpected had really, actually happened. He, the young, pleasure-loving dandy, the reckless worldling, the man without faith or stability—Traugott Gerrald—had repented, and was living quietly and respectably, industriously doing his duty.

"He is working like a lion!" exclaimed Baron Linden to his friends; and Lieutenant Horster said, regretfully:

"It's a pity; he was really a capital fellow. Well, we'll see how long his zeal will last."

The young ladies whispered secretly about the interesting Gerrald, who had actually been seen standing below at the door of the mill counting the sacks.

"How strange!" they giggled, and added a pitying: "Poor fellow! When one considers that he was called from the gaming-table to a death-bed, it was a hard lesson!"

Gerrald had no idea of the comments his worthy fellow-citizens were making upon him. Occupation was his sole thought. He now remembered that he owned large mills in the suburbs. He had seen them once as he rode by, very hastily, it is true, for at that time his mind was occupied with the beautiful ballet-dancer who had driven out in that direction. What had he cared for the mills then? He received the income from them, and often wondered why it grew smaller every year; but he had never thought of it long. Why should he? He had so many other things on his mind.

Now he recollected these mills, and much as he had formerly neglected them they now completely absorbed his attention.

He remembered that he had once been told that their management and oversight was in lax hands. He perceived that it was his duty to arrange and look after affairs there. He admitted that as owner and master he was responsible for his property.

He rode out that very day.

True, the men stared at him when he entered so resolutely to assert his rights as master. Most of them scarcely knew him, and the superintendent appeared by no means disposed to yield to him. He had probably formed quite a different idea of the owner from the man who stood so proudly before him, and was not prepared for the searching examination to which Gerrald subjected him.

A perfect chaos of fraud and embezzlement was revealed to Traugott's keen eyes. Imperfect, carelessly kept books and accounts greeted him with mute reproach; everywhere he encountered errors mistakes and neglect; wherever he turned, the work towered mountain high, and letters from creditors were heaped in packages upon the desk.

The mills consisted of a number of houses located at the end of the suburb. A large, square courtyard formed the center, surrounded by the homes of the laborers and the mill hands, whose lower stories contained the work-rooms, and closed on the east by the superintendent's house.

The employees were incited to open rebellion by this superintendent's representations.

"Who dares to contradict me here?" asked Gerrald's calm voice, rising above the murmurs of the men, who refused to work if any attempt was made to deprive them of their usual customs and privileges.

The rough figures pressed nearer to the young owner, who, leaning against the railing of the bridge over the mill-stream, fixed his stern eyes upon them.

"I!" shouted the superintendent. "We will not receive orders from a young man who scarcely knows himself how the work here is carried on. You have no idea of the business, Herr Gerrald, but you act as though we were all stupid apprentices compared with you, and must be intimidated and silenced by insolence. Do not imagine that you can accomplish anything of the sort with us! It is a great mistake. What do you want here, where I have managed matters until now?"

"What do I want?" Traugott retorted, with an annihilating glance. "I should think these books might answer."

He held up a bundle of books, which he had found in an utterly neglected condition.

"Where are the yearly accounts—the sales—the receipts? Is this the way to keep the books—to let the whole property go to ruin—and then ask impudently what the owner wants? Look at the stables yonder. They are falling to pieces, yet the money has been paid to put them in repair. What has become of it, superintendent? See the machines below—the condition in which you have left the warehouses. And how could you venture to sell any part of the ground without informing me? The payment is ludicrously small. You have given me an absurd price. I shall ascertain how much you actually received for the land."

The man advanced with arms akimbo.

"Pray inquire—accuse me—I shall know how to answer. But let me tell you this: In your father's lifetime neither the books nor the buildings were in any better condition, yet we made daily progress; but you, in your avarice, imagine that we might get a penny more here or there, and want to pry about yourself. But that doesn't suit us! We don't work under such control. We won't be spied upon, neither my men nor I. So decide whether you'll take yourself off again, and let everything go on as before, or whether we shall seek service elsewhere. You have only to choose."

"I stand on my own property, man," replied Traugott, calmly, "and affairs have really gone very far if I am to make way for my superintendent. I will not yield a single inch, and if that doesn't suit you, you are dismissed."

The superintendent's little eyes seamed fairly to devour Gerrald's tall figure.

"And what is to become of the mills, if there is no one to turn the wheels, eh?"

"That is my business," replied Traugott, shrugging his shoulders. "At any rate, I would rather close them than have you manage them another day."

"Well, then, you can all go to the tannery!" cried the superintendent, pale with fury. "There we shall find less niggardly masters and equally good wages."

"Indeed! Who told you so?" asked Gerrald, with folded arms. "I suppose you are not aware, men, that the tannery doesn't need another soul, and that there is an over-supply of workmen elsewhere?"

Already troubled faces appeared here and there,

and anxious whispers ran through the crowd as the men pressed impetuously nearer.

"What? What does he say?" called voices from the groups. "What is going on at the tannery?"

"It has failed!" replied Gerrald, loudly.

The men recoiled as if a thunderbolt had struck them.

"Don't believe it—he wants to frighten us!" shouted the superintendent. "The tannery stands better than any of the works here. See how the chimneys are pouring out smoke! Bird-lime, Sir Owner, bird-lime!"

"Hurrah, work is going on! Certainly it is!" called several voices from among the throng. And the men repeated their demands still more loudly and violently.

"You are discharged!" said Traugott, angrily. "But if any of you can read let him come forward."

A tall, pale-faced workman slowly advanced, scarcely daring to raise his eyes.

"Come, Lohfeld," repeated the young man, with a shade of reproach in his tone. "So I must see you, too, among the strikers, you whom my father always praised as an honest man?"

Lohfeld shrank, a deep blush crimsoned his face, and he glanced sullenly at his companions.

"They forced me to it, sir."

"Read his waste paper!" thundered the superintendent, advancing with clenched fists.

Traugott held out a document which he had just drawn from his breast-pocket.

The workman began to read with a trembling voice; his features grew paler and more agitated.

"Heavenly father, it has failed!"

"And here is the seal of the court," Gerrald continued calmly, holding the paper aloft. "The tannery has not been able to keep on with the business, and the creditors are pressing the sale. The magistrates offered it to me, and informed me of the matter first because the building could be conveniently incorporated with the mill here. Now go and seek employment. I need no men who wish to rebel against their master."

Lohfeld, deadly pale, approached, raising his clasped hands.

"Master!" he cried, frantically. "I have four children!"

"Have pity, master," pleaded a hundred voices; "almost all of us have families! Don't turn us off, or they must starve!"

Gerrald's stern expression vanished, and he held out his hand kindly to Lohfeld.

"No, my men, I will not make you homeless!" he called loudly. "Have no fear; I shall not plunge my workmen into poverty because, misled by unworthy men, they even desired a few minutes ago to deprive me of service and property. I have friends, manufacturers and owners of landed estates, with whom I will obtain places for you."

These few words had the effect of producing a tempest of emotion.

" No, master, we want to serve you. You are kinder than we have deserved!" they cried from overflowing hearts; and the men surrounded Gerrald, waving their caps. It was a beautiful spectacle to see the young owner of the mill, his face beaming with joy, as he shook hands with one after another weather-beaten figure.

The superintendent had slipped quietly away.

But the men confirmed their vows with a cordial clasp of the hand, and tears glittered in the eyes of many as their sinewy hands were raised to call down Heaven's blessings on their young master, while " Hurrah, hurrah for Herr Gerrald !" mingled joyously with the sound of the rippling waves of the mill-stream.

CHAPTER III.

HELOISE.

The purple curtains were closely drawn. The bright sunshine flickered over their folds and, casting a shining reflection upon the mirror-like floor, glided shimmering over the soft satin furniture and suffused the dancing *bayadere* with a roseate hue. Slender palms swayed above the elegant writing-desk, which was lavishly equipped with every trifle the nineteenth century gathers in a motley mosaic. Costly vases adorned the gilded shelves of the long pier-glasses; bald-headed Chinese gazed solemnly from gayly-painted boxes, and the azaleas blossoming in the niches in the walls contrasted, in their dreamy whiteness, with the chaos of costly articles huddled together upon the soft rugs.

Heloise, the reckless Frenchwoman, with a gay laugh ever on her lips, had already seen a great deal of the world. She had roamed hither and thither, dancing, laughing and rejoicing like the butterfly which sips the honey from every blossom.

So she had come to D—— and accepted an engagement at the court theatre. "Only for a few weeks," as she said, to comfort herself while passing through the quiet German city, imagining that she should die of *ennui;* but the result was quite different.

Heloise was amused by the universal idolatry bestowed upon her, and laughingly accepted the proofs of admiration; all were equally a matter of indifference to her, as well as the suitors for her favor, with the exception of one for whose coming she waited as the pilgrim in the desert watches for the drops of water; whose words made her happy as no other sound had ever done, yet who was only a plain young mill-owner, with neither lofty name nor position, though to her a god—omnipotent over her heart.

She loved, perhaps for the first time! Traugott Gerrald, handsome and full of life, was the first person who had fettered her coy heart, who had laughed and sung with her, and then so basely and suddenly deserted her for the sake of an old dead woman— his mother.

The bewitching dancer lay on the divan, half concealed by the waving palm-leaves, nestling among the cushions like a glittering adder sunning itself, rolled in a coil, amid the moss. Her little foot was angrily tossed upward, and the sharp heel of her morocco slipper kicked the gilded carving of the furniture as if it were the sole cause of her ill-humor. Then she sulkily turned page after page of the French novel, and finally, in a fit of sudden wrath, tossed it into the niche where the flowers stood. The white blossoms fell in a dense shower on the carpet, and the long-haired lap-dog fled, barking loudly, from its velvet cushions.

Heloise sprang up excitedly and paced swiftly through the drawing-room, her light morning-robe fluttered like an airy cloud around her full figure, and her embroidered flounces trailed over the floor. Folding her arms across her breast, with a gloomy look, she went to the writing-desk, and stood there pondering, with her little hands clenched as she gnawed her under-lip.

"If he doesn't come to-day, I'll write to him!" she muttered between her teeth. "Oh, it is really a pretty piece of business that he lets matters go so far that I, the sovereign, the omnipotent queen, must sue for his presence! Yet do I really love him? Love him? It almost seems so, yet it should not, must not be!"

Just at that moment the *portière* rustled; the dancer started, pressing her hand upon her heart; the door opened, and her maid's fair locks appeared between the heavy folds.

"Mademoiselle, this bouquet—"

In two paces Heloise was standing at her side, and hastily snatched the flowers out of her hand.

"From whom?" fell breathlessly from her lips.

"Herr Lieutenant Horster presents his compliments—"

"Silence!" thundered the Frenchwoman, hurling the bouquet violently on the floor. "I am at home to no one to-day; no one, do you hear? I have a headache; I am ill. Yet stay—if Herr Gerrald—"

"Ah!" nodded Susanne, significantly, with a slight expression of sarcasm hovering about her thin lips. "Is Herr Gerrald coming again at last?"

"That is no affair of yours," replied the dancer, haughtily. "Don't forget the position you occupy in my service; a maid must keep silent or curb her saucy tongue, or she will be dismissed. Note that and go!" She waved her hand toward the door. "Or stop—" She went to the writing-desk and hurriedly scrawled a few lines on a sheet of paper, put it into an envelope and gave it to the maid. "Find a messenger, Susanne, and have this letter taken to Herr Gerrald at once."

Young Gerrald was standing below in the arched stone doorway, watching the wagons, loaded with grain, which rolled creaking over the flag-stones, when Heloise's note was delivered to him. He glanced quietly at the hurried address, a swift, burning blush crimsoned his brow, and he put the missive into his pocket.

" Thank you ; it needs no answer.

" Lohfeld, the next wagon is coming from the store-houses ; how many hundred-weight have you calculated ?"

" One hundred and sixty-three, master," replied the new superintendent, rapidly adding the figures; " twenty-five from the city, and the hundred and thirty-eight from Dornhof make in all one hundred and sixty-three."

Lohfeld went down to the work-rooms, and the gray horses vanished in the stable ; everything grew quiet about the young master of the mill.

He still leaned against the stone gateway, his glance wandering over the spacious courtyard, which, full of life and labor, had become his proud domain. Happiness, quiet, elevating happiness took possession of him, and he almost shuddered at the thought of the past which he had so uselessly wasted, of which he had robbed himself. Like a flash of lightning the beautiful woman rose before his soul, radiant, gay and faithless as the dragon-fly hovering over the rippling surface of the water.

Smiling almost contemptuously, he drew the perfumed note from his pocket, and the lines which a

The Opposite House. 29

few weeks before would have elevated him to the skies, which he would probably have longed to frame like a jewel in gold, he now touched with the tips of his fingers, reluctantly, timidly, as if the little flourishing letters burned like fire.

"Gerrald," ran the lines, "another week has passed without any news, any sign of life from you. Tyrant, do you wish to force me to beg for your presence? *Oh, you men are terrible, when you know that you are beloved.* I respect your grief for Frau Gertrude, but its duration is wearisome. It cannot help the dead, and it troubles me. You wish suddenly to play virtuous, as people say. Nay, you even count the meal-bags! Do not make yourself ridiculous by an idea which, in a short time, will seem horribly stupid. Consider your beautiful hands. If you will not be sensible, be vain. And—don't be tiresome, Gerrald. I hate tiresome people. Come to me—at once. *Au revoir, mon cher.* Bring me a smile! HELOISE."

A gloomy frown darkened his brow, his blue eyes flashed contemptuously, almost angrily as they rested on the lines. The familiar tone, the frivolous judgment of his improvement, wounded him to the very depths of his soul. Good heavens! And he might have loved this woman! Loved her, about whom there was nothing true or genuine, except the levity under the rouge.

He drew himself up proudly. His slender figure seemed to grow with the long breath that expanded his chest, and slowly, with almost contemptuous composure, he tore up the little note. Scrap after scrap fluttered down into the rippling mill-stream, and the waves sportively bore them away. He watched them as they vanished in the white foam or were tossed upward till they finally sank out of sight.

With a quiet smile he laid his hand upon his heart, where the white flower of death rested, and full of noble resolution, raised his eyes to the blue spring heavens.

"I must and will go to her once more to destroy this delusion forever."

He crossed the courtyard in the direction of the stables.

"Josef, is my break ready?"

"Yes, Herr Gerrald," and the groom pushed the light vehicle out of the carriage-house.

Traugott went to his dun horses, adjusted the reins on their slender necks, stroked their shining sides caressingly, and led them out in front of the high vehicle, into which he sprang with a bound.

"Josef, go over to the superintendent and order— Ah, Lohfeld!"

The latter was just coming from the store-houses with a long list in his hand.

"You called me, master?" he said, hurrying forward. "Are there any orders for the afternoon?"

Traugott lighted his cigar and flung down the match.

"No; but the letters on my desk are to be mailed,

and if the head of the office comes from Dornhof, you know where I am to be found. That's all for to-day. I must go up to the city and open the windows in the old house."

He took up the reins and returned the bows of the two employees. Then the impatient horses started, and the equipage flew as swiftly along the high road to D—— as the light clouds flit across the sky.

CHAPTER IV.

TWO GABLE HOUSES.

The Gerrald house stood in the center of the city. The street was one of those ancient ones, a relic of bygone days, when dignified members of the senate passed along, litters and clumsy coaches swayed to and fro, or fair, girlish faces peeped through the leaden-cased panes, to drop at the feet of the *Raths-herr* a sprig of rosemary, which in the good old days meant, in the language of the flowers: "I will go with you to the altar."

Here on the stone door-post still stood a large " L. G.," and below, nearly obliterated, " 1673," that were meant for old Leopold Gerrald, the haughty, morose gentleman in black-velvet blouse and huge lace collar, who for a long time occupied a seat in the senate, and with dignified bearing marched at the head of the guild. His portrait still hung in the hall. Here a delicate coat of arms was traced—a leaping horse and an empty field beneath. It was probably done by handsome Zacharias Gerrald's wild son, who was angry because his pale mother was a Von Rotterswyl, and who went with his brother to the field as a bold cuirassier to fight the insolent Swedes. This Deithelm had fled from home because he had stabbed his mother's proud nephew, Baron von Rotterswyl, in a duel. Those were gloomy days.

On the other side of the way, another gable house, equally old, worm-eaten and weather-worn, leaned toward its smaller neighbors, which, crowded closely together, formed the narrow street. A stone staircase led up to the arched door, above whose carved top was a huge gray escutcheon—a leaping horse and an empty field beneath.

It was the home of the Barons von Rotterswyl.

The two houses had faced each other for centuries, both equally ancient and venerated. Around the one with the coronet hovered the halo of a noble name. The other bore the praiseworthy crown of labor. Yet their aspect was as cold and hostile as though the narrow street were a yawning chasm, which neither bridge nor friendship could unite.

It had been different once. Then nobleman and merchant clasped hands with fraternal affection. Then handsome Zacharias daily visited the house with the gray escutcheon and sat at the carved oaken table opposite to the master of the house to pledge him from an ancient beaker. Doubtless a sincere friendship united the families until the bitter hour when the baron's high-born daughter fled to the house of the plebeian merchant, and with each fatal step thrust the swaying bridge down into the black abyss.

Ay, the old ancestral portraits in the neighboring house could tell long stories of that unhappy time, bloody tales of hate, enmity and scorn, which the son inherited from the father. The feud was persistently maintained to punish the insolence, and a barrier was erected between the two houses which not even centuries could overthrow.

Marie von Rotterswyl, the daughter of the old baroness, occupied the bow-window above. This was her chosen kingdom, among the flowers and twittering birds, where she could follow the dictates of every passing mood, rejoice with the glad sunshine or sit lost in reverie for hours before the dark oil-painting which, removed from the portrait gallery, was banished to this room under the roof.

Marie knew the story of her ancestress; she had often heard her mentioned, with bitter rancor, as the only blot upon the stainless genealogy. Full of intense sympathy, Marie had carried the portrait of the exile to her little bow-windowed room, carefully wiped the cobwebs and dust from the dark frame and concealed it like a beloved and precious treasure behind her flowers.

Marie was still scarcely more than a child, though she had seen sixteen springs. But, secluded from the outside world, untouched by its poisonous breath, she had bloomed like a lily of the field, unconscious of her own beauty.

Tall and slender, with bewitching grace in every movement, she resembled the poetic ideal of the German maiden. Thick waves of golden hair were gathered into a knot, and light curls framed a white brow, beneath which laughed eyes as blue and radiant as a bit of the spring sky reflected in a still forest lake.

Marie was again standing with clasped hands and lowered lashes before the portrait of her pale ancestress; some incomprehensible attraction seemed to draw her as if by magic to the face which gazed down at her so tenderly and sadly.

"Do I really look like her?" she asked herself, thoughtfully. "Aunt Verja says so. I am younger, far younger; but she, too, was once sixteen, and before she had wept and suffered so much, her cheeks were perhaps more rosy. You were right, Ancestress Barbara, and I—I would do the same! What do I care for all the coronets and coats of arms, all the proud names which sound so cold, so repellent? What do I care for a mother who loves nothing but her family, and lets her own child pine for its sake? You, Barbara, are the only one who understands me, who knows how it hurts to have no heart in the breast; nothing but an escutcheon, where other people can love and feel! You have loved, and you were happy! Isn't mamma wrong, Ancestress Barbara, when she says: 'Love is an illusion, but noble blood is a sacred possession?'" And drawing a long breath, Marie pushed her fair locks back from her brow and turned toward the window. "Who knows, perhaps she occupied my little room up here and handsome Zacharias Gerrald looked out of the opposite window—"

She did not finish the sentence, but, with sudden terror, bent over her roses and gazed across at the merchant's house, at whose window she saw a stranger, whose face was handsomer and more attractive than any which she had ever beheld. Locks of fair hair clustered thickly over his brow, and his dark eyes were fixed mournfully on the sky—Traugott Gerrald.

He turned his head—his glance wandered to the gray house, rested on the window filled with roses, and, starting in astonishment, he stared at the lovely little face, whose large blue eyes were fixed so timidly and inquiringly upon him. His own eyes grew brighter, the flush on his brow deeper. Who was she?

Their glances met only for a moment; then the golden-haired child suddenly started, the rose petals fell to the floor in a shower, the white curtain shook; but she had vanished, and he saw nothing except the rigid features of a portrait hanging on the wall. Was he excited, or was he the sport of some spectral illusion? The portrait seemed to raise its white hands and, with a beseeching gesture, wave the young man back. What did you fear, Barbara von Rotterswyl?

*   *   *   *   *   *

Gerrald stood at the window half an hour longer, staring fixedly at the baronial house, as if he hoped the weather-beaten stones would open and afford him another glimpse of the vision which had so surprised him that he could scarcely appreciate the details of its beauty. But, like the elusive *Fata Morgana*, the sunny phantom of the desert, the apparition had vanished behind the rose-bushes, leaving him nothing save the ugly, bare reality—the empty window in the house of a hostile family. No golden locks glimmered through the green foliage, and the lovely eyes and swift smile had disappeared as completely as if he had never seen them.

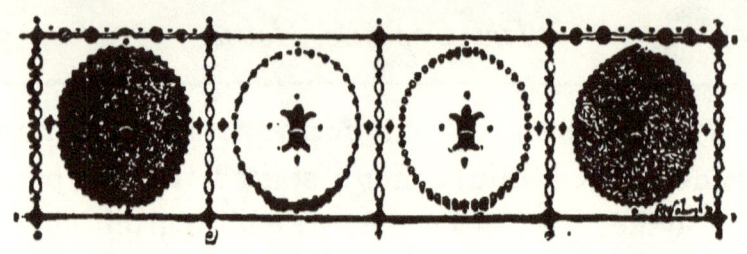

CHAPTER V.

THE TALISMAN.

Traugott walked rapidly down the street, without casting a glance upward at the window of the young baroness, amid whose green leafage a finch was carolling its vesper song; his eyes were bent upon the stone flags of the pavement, and he imagined that, in every crevice, he saw the sneering face of the old baroness, the woman to whom all that bore the name of Gerrald had no existence! But Marie? Did those loving child-like eyes know the insolent language of arrogance? Could they coldly, heartlessly, see nothing save that blot upon the ancient name, and condemn the family whose great-grandfather had been preferred to a coat of arms? Had those sweet lips been taught to utter bitter words against the hated neighbor, the little golden head pondered over those horrible scenes of the past, in which an unfortunate sword-thrust made the nephew the murderer of his aristocratic uncle? And yet—might it not have been merely a fateful accident that she bestowed the sunny smile on a Gerrald? Had the blush and hasty retreat aught to do with him?

Traugott rushed into the main street; he wanted to see and hear his fellow-mortals. What interest should he feel in this aristocrat, who was also his enemy, and whom he had seen scarcely a moment? But how did it happen that he had never seen her before? Before! When did he come home in former days? Perhaps at midnight, when those sweet eyes had long been closed in sleep, when she had probably murmured a little prayer under the portrait of her despised ancestress, perchance besought mercy for all souls that were in evil paths and thus unconsciously for him, who, at this time, was throwing away his money on the green table or languishing at the feet of that frivolous Frenchwoman.

An impetuous desire seized upon the young man with overwhelming might:

"To Heloise! I'll show her that I was a fool in those days!"

He swiftly traversed the few intervening streets, and again stood before the door of the house in which he had formerly been a daily guest. Before ringing the bell he paused a moment, raised his hat, and let the cool evening breeze fan his burning brow caressingly.

The bell pealed shrilly through the corridor; light steps approached the door. Susanne fairly started back:

"You, Herr Gerrald?"

"Yes, I," he answered curtly. "Is mademoiselle at home?"

The girl flew rather than walked over the soft carpet back to her mistress. A loud exclamation, which sounded almost like a cry of delight, reached his ears; then Susanne returned and threw the door wide open:

"Mademoiselle Heloise is dressing for the opera, but will come presently."

Gerrald again stood in the little *boudoir* which had formerly seemed to him an Elysium. She had so often reclined in yonder chair, while, kneeling on a cushion at her side, he talked about eternal love. Folly! The sweet odor of heliotrope seemed to oppress his breathing; the magical dusk, the embers glimmering on the hearth, the heavy fragrance of the flowers—all combined to stupefy his senses. He felt too weak to cope with this task. If only she did not keep him waiting too long, the delay was so tiresome. He was about to seek refuge in flight—his hand already grasped the velvet *portière*—when the vision in the bow-window rose before him, and he felt as though panoplied by the memory of the innocent girl behind the laughing roses, innocent of deception, rouge or guile, herself as fair as a flower; and, drawing a long sigh of relief, he remained. Several minutes passed; then the door opened softly, a flood of brilliant light poured into the little room and, glittering like a dragon-fly, laughing, scantily clad in ballet-costume, the bewitching Heloise rushed to meet him.

Traugott involuntarily stepped back; the flood of light dazzled him, and he pressed his hand almost timidly upon his breast, on the white blossom he wore on his heart. Heloise was indeed beautiful—fairer, more bewitching than ever.

Smiling radiantly as of yore, she stood before him with arms uplifted. Then she sank lightly on one knee, the glittering gauze dress floating about her like a golden cloud:

"My lord—my loved one!" The head, crowned with dark curls, drooped upon her breast, the white arms were folded across the shimmering gauze. The tableau was fascinating and cleverly planned.

Traugott slowly approached her.

"Mademoiselle—"

Heloise raised her eyes in astonishment; then, laughing merrily, she started up and clung closely to him.

"No, Gerrald!" she exclaimed with beaming eyes.

"Let this cruel sport end now, and be once more the sensible, gay Gerrald of former days. You see your success; you perceive that I have been forced to recall you; that I have knelt at your feet to honor you as an omnipotent master. What more do you want, now that you know that I love you?" The dark eyes gazed at him with an alluring smile, and the snowy arms clasped his neck. "Have you entirely forgotten the happy past, Traugott?"

He wrenched himself from her embrace and stepped back.

"Certainly, I have forgotten it, Mademoiselle Chênois. When we wear crape on the arms, we no longer think of days which make a serious man— blush."

Heloise started back; an angry flash darted from her sparkling eyes.

"It seems you wish to preach virtue!" she answered mockingly. "Ha, ha, ha! Don't you remember how you taught me the most charming drinking songs, and joined the most gayly in the chorus?" And swaying lightly forward from the waist she hummed the tune.

Traugott gazed gloomily at the floor.

"No, Heloise," he said gravely. "Cease this jesting with a man on whom grief inflicted deep wounds only a few weeks ago. I have come to-day to bid you farewell forever; our paths in life are too unlike to be united. You are the careless child of the South, who must always laugh, sing and dance; but I have become a man. I have had my days of pleasure; perhaps devoted myself too completely to it. Now all that is over, and my future watchword is 'Duty,' which is more sacred to me than all the thousand hours which I dreamed away in your arms—at your feet. I am no longer the Traugott Gerrald of former days; no longer the easily captivated boy. I have become my own master, and must give an account of my deeds and conduct to myself and to my beloved dead."

The dancer looked at him with an expression of mingled pity and derision.

"So you have really taken Madam Gertrude's death so much to heart? Good heavens, what a contrast to the way in which you regarded it a few weeks ago! Then the aforesaid lady was the only obstacle to our union. I could almost admire your grief and energy, if they were only applied to a different purpose; *quelle horreur* to be such a Prince of the Mill, as people nickname you, forever among meal-bags. Ha, ha, ha!"

She fairly shook with laughter, and was charming in this mood also.

Traugott's face crimsoned to the very brow.

"You sneer at me for having begun to work and learned to despise myself. I regret that I let matters go so far that I am forced to be ashamed of those days."

He nodded, and turned his back upon her; but ere he could reach the *portières*, an airy cloud fluttered into his path. Heloise sank between the heavy velvet folds.

"No, do not go too far, Gerrald!" she cried, beseechingly. "I have endured your rudeness with rare patience, a proof of my infinite love. You must not leave me thus, in anger! Only one look into my eyes; just one. Traugott, tell me that you are not angry with me; that you will come again. One word, only one word, Gerrald, or you will drive me mad!"

She was a brilliant actress, every one admitted, and could throw a world of expression into her eyes. It was so now. She gazed at him with infinite anxiety. Her dark curls fell low on her brow; magnificent diamonds glittered amid their thick masses; her rosy arms held the heavy folds closely together. Nothing but force could part them. Traugott drew back a step, and almost involuntarily fixed his enraptured eyes upon the fascinating creature who knelt at his feet, more beautiful than ever.

She raised her clasped hands; her glance sought his, timidly, beseechingly; and as he saw her thus before him, the features, which were once his all, as beautiful, as enthralling as ever, a flood of consuming fire seemed to seethe in his heart and bewilder his soul; the old wound opened, and an irresistible attraction drew him to the bewitching creature. He was on the point of rushing toward her and clasping her with passionate fervor to his breast, kneeling at her feet to plead for pardon, love and happiness, when he felt a sharp, sudden pang, and pressing his hand upon his breast, touched the gold locket and his mother's white flower of death.

A tremor ran through every limb; his foot paused and his hands fell loosely at his side; deadly pale, but calm and cold as stone, he drew back. The spell was broken.

Heloise had noted everything. What did he wear on his heart? "It must be dear to him, dearer and more precious than I." This thought darted wildly through her brain, and she slowly rose.

"You no longer love me, Gerrald. I see that. But I do not yet know what has captured your fancy."

Her eyes glittered like those of a beast of prey watching for its booty. What did he wear on his heart? She was determined to learn at any cost, and slowly approached him.

"Show me what you have hidden there, and I will release you."

He gazed at her in stern astonishment; then, smiling calmly, held up the gold case.

"My talisman, my sacred legacy. So long as I possess it, I am panoplied against you!"

One more look at the radiant creature—it would be the last—and his steps died away on the soft carpet. But the laughing butterfly within the room raised her clenched right hand and, from the depths of her sorely wounded heart, muttered a fierce: "Revenge!"

CHAPTER VI.

MEPHISTOPHELES.

Traugott Gerrald was seated in his light carriage, driving to D——, impatiently, almost feverishly, longing to see his golden-haired neighbor across the street. Fragrant blossoms laughed around him, thousands of buds smiling with their bright eyes at the beautiful world around them; the air echoed with the jubilant gladness of spring; hundreds of feathered songsters were greeting their old home with joyous melodies. At one side of the road the mill-stream was dancing through the waving grass, plashing saucily over the sharp stones which opposed its course, and around which the forget-me-not twined its slender arms. Bright butterflies flew hither and thither on fluttering wings; glittering flies danced above the waves; fleecy white clouds were reflected in them. The whole world was radiant with the sunny spring.

Almost involuntarily Traugott drew in his reins and raised his hat. The freshness seemed to enter his very heart, and he smiled as he watched the play of two swallows, darting in zig-zag lines through the blue air, eluding, yet at last joining each other.

At the same moment he heard behind him the rapid beat of a horse's hoofs. A man was urging a snorting steed down the highway.

"Strange," thought Traugott, "he dashes along like the Wild Huntsman himself;" and he turned his own horses aside to make room for the unknown rider.

But the latter seemed to have other intentions. Stopping beside Traugott's vehicle, he raised his hat courteously:

"Have I the pleasure of speaking to Herr Gerrald?"

Traugott, much surprised, returned the bow.

"Yes, my name is Gerrald!"

"I am delighted to meet you," the stranger continued. "I have come directly from the mills, where I learned you had already left your rooms. I wished to do myself the honor of renewing a very slight acquaintance and paying you a visit."

"I really don't know—I am extremely sorry; but I cannot possibly recall—" stammered the young owner of the mills. The pale face, with its piercing eyes and perpetual smile, seemed familiar.

"My name is Brand—Doctor Brand," said the horseman, courteously, introducing himself. "You will hardly remember me, as I, unfortunately, merely had the pleasure of a casual introduction at Wiesbaden."

"And what procures me the honor now?" Traugott's features had become cold and proud,

"I came here to examine D—— thoroughly, and, in case it should suit me, make it my residence," the doctor continued. "Unfortunately, I am a total stranger, and would consider myself fortunate to meet an acquaintance who would have the kindness to give me a little information about various matters. Your name was the only one known to me, so, perhaps, my advance is from very selfish motives."

"I fear that I can be of no special assistance to you," replied Gerrald, with courteous reserve. "I mean so far as introducing you into society here. I rarely go out now—and—"

"Would prefer, to speak frankly, to have no relations with me?" interrupted Brand, smiling, though his keen eyes seemed to pierce the young man's inmost heart. "Oh, Gerrald!" he continued, while a shadow flitted over his face, "there was, indeed, once a time of which I am ashamed, and which justifies the distrust you show me, a period you also have experienced—I mean the gaming-tables at Wiesbaden. I looked on there while, by my side, you undermined your fortune; rushed with open eyes to meet ruin, and felt in the depths of my heart that I ought to guard you, consider your youth, and warn you against approaching disaster. I felt this, yet kept silence. You look at me sullenly, Gerrald. Why are you in such sudden haste? No, listen; I must make this confession."

He seized Traugott's reins with an iron hand, and, checking the impatient horses, continued:

"I watched you gamble for three successive evenings, sympathized with you, was interested in your appearance. It is foolish to say that at the gaming-table nothing is seen and heard save the demon of gold; on the contrary, I was never passionately fond of play. I took part in it merely to see and study others. It was so in your case. Your personal appearance attracted me; your youth awakened my sympathy; you seemed to me an unusual character. It was probably the first time you had gambled; there was still opportunity for a friendly hand to hold you back; but you, yourself, know the world, the egotistical, careless world, which has so few weak moments. 'What is it to me?' said a cruel voice in my heart. 'Why do you meddle with other people's affairs to receive ingratitude and rebuffs in return for your good-will?' I looked on as you lost, saw one bank-note after another go to the croupier—looked on in silence. So matters went until you ceased to come. It ought to have been a matter of indifference to me. Why should I care whether you appeared or not? But I seemed to miss something at the green-table. I missed my evening amusement—I was bored. As though forced by some invisible power, I was compelled to follow you here, Gerrald; hear and speak to you, know you better. Do you think me an eccentric fellow? There must be such characters. Yet be assured that my meaning is sincere and honest when I offer my hand in friendship."

There was a strange spell in this man's voice; its tones were captivating and full of sincerity.

Traugott clasped his proffered hand, but his manner still showed the same reserve as he replied:

"You are welcome, doctor. I am now alone and friendless, and therefore feel doubly grateful for every token of sympathy. The past which you have just mentioned is only a brief, dark scene, which must be swallowed up in the present. Work, exertion, occupation make me happy; and when you see for yourself what new triumphs I am daily achieving, you will understand what an ennobling feeling it is to be able to say: 'This is my work, for whose sake I have toiled and struggled.'"

Brand nodded silently. His face at that moment wore quite a different expression than usual. Doctor Brand's appearance was remarkable. His countenance, though not ugly, had a look which unconsciously inspired fear. Narrow, colorless, with a perpetual smile resting on the thin lips, it produced the impression of a white plaster cast, on whose temples two blue veins have been drawn. Only the deep-set eyes gave life, a strange, wavering life, to the face. Young girls shunned him, women usually disliked him, but men laughed at both and declared that the doctor was an unusually interesting and agreeable man. True, there were some sharp tongues among them which said that Brand might have served as a model when Kaulbach sketched his Mephistopheles.

The doctor resumed the conversation.

"You are a happy man, and that is enviable; but you lack one thing."

"What may that be?" asked Traugott, smiling.

"A wife, a loyal and beautiful companion for life. Tell me, Gerrald, do you wish to live for yourself alone? Whenever I have thought of you, I have always imagined an ideal maiden at your side."

Traugott smiled mournfully.

"I have much to accomplish ere I can win her."

A swift glance flashed across Brand's face, the glance of an adder, which sees its victim in the distance:

"Then you know where to turn to obtain her? It seems to me that you have already chosen!"

The road led down a slight hill, and Gerrald stooped forward to use the brake; it was probably the bending posture which sent the blood to his face.

"I? Whom should I choose?"

"Listen, my young friend," Brand replied, insinuatingly, leaning closer to him. "There are rumors in town of a love affair with the Chênois. Is there any truth in the gossip?"

Traugott started as though the pale face was a viper, hissing at him with sparkling eyes.

"No, no," he vehemently exclaimed; "a thousand times no! Who has dared to say so? True, I once paid homage to her, because I was a boy who could be dazzled by the glitter of tinsel; now everything is at an end between us, and I hope I shall never again be placed in the embarrassing position of being compelled to meet the lady."

The doctor smiled—a disagreeable smile—then suddenly turned his horse to the side of the road. A carriage was just dashing by, from which a head, covered with dark curls, bent forward, and a pair of sparkling eyes gazed at the two gentlemen with a strangely earnest expression—a look as swift and keen as a flash of lightning met Brand's glance. He answered it with the same quickness and sharpness, then the equipage vanished in clouds of dust.

A short distance farther brought them to the

street in which stood the two ancient gable-houses, and Traugott stopped before his own door.

"Do you live here?" cried Brand, scanning the building with a hasty glance. "An interesting old edifice! I suppose the arrangement is still unchanged? I am extravagantly fond of such things, and even had a great desire to become an architect; but, unluckily, my father put too many difficulties in the way. Yes, my dear Gerrald, you must allow me to see it some day. No, thank you, not now," he added, as Traugott, with a courteous gesture, invited him to dismount. "Not to-day; but I will come again soon, if you will allow me. Magnificent, matchless stone-carving! *Au revoir*, my dear friend. I congratulate you on possessing so pleasant a home." He pressed his hand cordially. "Farewell!"

He had a pleasant way of taking leave which could not fail to produce an agreeable impression. Traugott thoughtfully ascended the stairs and entered his room.

The white curtain at the window opposite waved slightly, and the boughs of the rose-bushes were swaying to and fro. Traugott hastily approached and greeted his Gretchen with a radiant glance, while in the street below a black steed, swiftly and noiselessly as the wind, was bearing back to the highway its rider—Mephistopheles.

CHAPTER VII.

A MEETING.

A year had passed.

Twilight has gathered in Marie's little room. Deep shadows veil the fragrant blossoms of the monthly roses, and the darkness has lulled the feathered songsters to rest. Little can be seen of the faded splendor of the old-fashioned articles garnered in every corner with loving care; even the portrait of Ancestress Barbara seems to be veiled with gray gauze, and the eyes alone gaze down like two black spots upon the fair descendant who, lost in thought, sits with her head resting on her hand among the roses.

Marie had thrown on a dark morning wrapper; her fair braids hung half disheveled down her back. Have you ever chanced to see the picture of the "Sister of Charity" watching beside the couch of the young warrior, dear reader? The face of the youthful Baroness von Rotterswyl wore the same calm, pure, devout expression. She was thinking. What was the subject of her reverie? The roses poured forth a fragrance as exquisite as if they could guess her thoughts, bent low over the girl's golden head, and whispered into her ears happy ideas of love and the fresh foliage of spring, of the handsome man who lived in the house opposite, and who had such sparkling eyes and so lofty a brow—the man who stood so long at the window to catch a glance from her, and who absorbed all her thoughts, whose name was Gerrald, and whom her mother hated because he bore it!

Just at that moment the door softly opened, a flood of lamplight streamed into the little room, and Marie suddenly started up and took a few steps toward the door:

"Oh, it is you, Aunt Verja!"

A woman's slender figure glided into the little room, and, holding the lamp aloft, exclaimed, in clear musical tones:

"Aha, here is our little enthusiast! Yes, just as I imagined, alone among the roses, in a dark room. Good heavens, my dear, what a pity that I didn't bring some gentlemen with me; there would be a dozen duels to-morrow on account of this charming idyl! But your house is too horribly dark. I don't understand how you can stand it, child. I should have been frightened to death long ago."

She set the lamp on the table and flung her elegant shawl on the nearest chair, then eagerly put her arm around the young girl and kissed her rosy cheeks.

"You dear aunt," replied Marie, tenderly, "have you climbed all these stairs to my hermitage? I rarely have any visitors here, and am doubly glad to welcome you."

"I wanted to see your sanctum once," said the lady, laughing, as she tossed her fan and gloves on the chair too. "I have heard you talk of this cabinet of curiosities so often, without ever gaining admittance to it. Your mamma was not in the drawing-room, so I took a lamp and made my way up here. You know I never stop to consider long. What should I have done without a lamp! Don't be vexed, Marie, but I think your house is a terrible place. These stairs and corners and towers and bow-windows! Every time I bumped against some treacherous beam or cupboard I thanked Providence that I didn't live here." Panting for breath, she dropped into a chair and drew Marie down upon the stool at her side.

Aunt Verja was a wonderfully pretty woman—a thorough Russian, from the crown of her head to the tips of her dainty feet. A piquant, narrow little face, with a pale complexion, as transparently delicate as the petal of a flower, and with the creamy hue so beautiful in Oriental women—a face to which the slight arch of the nose gave an expression of character. The eyes were large and bright—sparkling, yet often dreamy; veiled, as it were, by bewitching melancholy, then sparkling with sudden passion. The delicately outlined brows harmonized with the scarlet lips, which, curled as if in mockery, revealed the little white teeth; a mischievous expression often hovered around them; pouting and drollery alternated with every shade of emotion.

"A clever, interesting woman!" was the verdict of D——, whose society people could not sufficiently praise the beauty of the young baroness. "A little spitfire, full of delightful caprices!" was probably added, and then the thousand and one charming bits of mischief which she so well understood how to enact were repeated.

Verja lived in very handsome style. She had married Frau von Rotterswyl's youngest brother, his highness's adjutant, Baron von Kartegg, who idolized his charming wife and made her the star and center of society in D——.

"Do you know, Marie," said the young aunt, laughing, "that I had quite an interesting experience a short time ago? Just think, a few weeks since Herr von Esen presented to me a young doctor of laws, black and white as marble—very brilliant effect—and who can talk, oh, wonderfully! I conversed with him for half an hour, and regretted that I must stop for propriety's sake. It's a pity that his name is merely Brand and the clever fellow doesn't belong to the nobility."

Marie had listened breathlessly.

"And does this doctor ride, aunt?" she asked, with glowing cheeks.

"Certainly; and he is a very striking figure when he dashes by on his splendid horse. He knows it, too. 'Pluto is the marrow of my life!' he said himself."

Marie was of a different opinion. She shuddered whenever she saw him at Gerrald's side, yet she did not know why.

"I should like to see him again," Verja eagerly went on. "I *must* see him for certain reasons, but where? But stay—he rides to the Gerrald mills every day at three o'clock to see young Gerrald! By the way, it must be a year now since the latter's mother died; he'll probably shake off his mourning all the more suddenly now, because he is such an odd fellow. How quickly time passes! I'll tell you, Marie, we'll go out to drive at three o'clock to-morrow; you'll accompany me, won't you, pet? I'll call for you in my pony carriage, and we'll drive to the mills. The road is said to be very pretty; at least perfectly shaded. Be ready at the exact hour. I should be frantic if we missed him."

Frau von Kartegg released Marie from her embrace and glanced hastily at the clock, then rushed to the chair and wrapped the shawl around her beautiful shoulders.

"Will you go to the opera with me, Marie? There is a vacant seat in our box. It is 'Tannhäuser.'"

"Not this evening, aunt; some other time."

"As you choose, pet. Meanwhile, I'll tell your mother that it is time for you to make your entrance into society. To-morrow at three, then? My lord and master sends his kindest remembrances to you. He has gone with Prince George to G——, or he would have come with me. So good-by, and be sure to be punctual."

Then the slender figure glided out of the room, Marie following with the lamp. The old house was too full of nooks and corners. But the moonbeams stole through the window and quivered over the roses, which poured forth an almost stupefying perfume as they bent whispering toward the ancient portrait, which gazed down at them with a proud smile.

* * * * * *

It is delightful to dash through the bright sunshine, vying with the birds, whose broad pinions cleave the blue air as they soar joyously to the light spring clouds; delightful to have the aromatic air fan the brow caressingly, banishing all dark thoughts and fancies.

Marie had leaned back in the carriage and, with eyes half closed, was dreaming amid all this splendor of another happiness, far brighter and more divine, whose radiant sun is called Love, and which hides behind many a cloud gathered by grief and longing.

Verja could not keep quiet. Her whole nature rebelled against meditation, and to be wholly alone with one's own thoughts appeared to her the most tiresome occupation possible for a human being. Even now her dark eyes were roving eagerly over the broad plains, sometimes kindling with sudden interest, sometimes resting wearily on the green tree-tops.

Opening and closing her elegant fan excitedly, she half turned back in her seat, saying:

"It's too bad; half-past three already, and nothing in sight. Jonas, walk the horses. Oh, Marie, I should be frantic, miserable, if he did not come. I have a plan for introducing Brand into society at court, spite of his plebeian birth. I've so set my heart upon it and arranged everything so cleverly, nothing would induce me to give it up. Dear me! No, it isn't he!" She angrily averted her head. "I almost mistook a market-wagon for the clever Brand."

Marie began to laugh.

"You are certainly very much excited, dear aunt," she said, in a jesting tone. "How can you think of society amid this beautiful scenery?"

"Oh, nonsense about nature!" replied Frau von Kartegg. "I don't understand how you can feel so little interest. I assure you that I shall have no peace until the doctor sits beside me at the princess's *musicale*, and if I turn D—— upside down, I will accomplish my purpose."

She pouted with an air of the most charming defiance, and shielded her eyes from the sunbeams with her fan.

"Where was this famous personage all last summer?" asked Marie. "I didn't see him ride by at all for a time, and he was often absent weeks."

"He travelled a great deal," replied Verja, absently, "but now he intends to remain here entirely." She bent sideways a little. "Marie!"—she clutched her niece's hand with an iron grasp—"look there—over yonder—two horsemen."

The young baroness started.

"*Two* horsemen?" she slowly repeated. "I thought you expected no one but the doctor?"

"Yes, yes," cried Verja, raising her lorgnette, "the other must be young Gerrald himself. Look again, and don't be so tiresome — quick, Marie. Well?"

The young girl, trembling, bent forward from the carriage.

"I don't know either of them," she said, without reflecting how the vivid flush which crimsoned her cheeks belied her words. Verja was too much absorbed by her own thoughts to notice it.

"Lean back!" she said, smiling. "One, two— you must bow when I do. Will you remember, *petite?*" She leaned carelessly among the cushions and seemed to be thinking only of her fan, which she negligently opened and shut, or balanced on her finger. Marie scarcely dared to breathe. The horsemen slowly approached—the carriage-horses were walking.

The fair-haired man started and gazed silently at the lovely little face. How quickly the expression of his features changed, gaining new life! Marie timidly raised her long lashes, and for an instant their eyes met.

Doctor Brand cast a swift glance at his companion, smiled—and raised his hat. Meanwhile, Verja's fan slipped from her hand and fell into the road. Brand, with a hasty movement, turned Pluto and reached the carriage-door, exclaiming:

"Your fan, madam." Then, with the speed of thought, he sprang from the saddle, raised the lost article, and, bowing courteously, presented it to the owner.

Verja thanked him gayly:

"Just think, my dear doctor, I didn't recognize you, spite of my good eyes and the broad daylight."

Brand had remounted and turned his horse.

"You are very kind, baroness!" he answered very chivalrously. "It is honor enough to occupy a small place in your memory. If you will permit me, I will venture to strengthen it by keeping my position here at your side."

"Certainly," said the Russian, nodding a gracious assent; "it will be a thousand times more entertaining to have some society while pursuing this monotonous road, that we may at least exchange thoughts. Permit me to make you acquainted with my niece, Doctor Brand—Fräulein von Rotterswyl."

Both bowed silently, then Brand asked if he might present his companion, and in response to Verja's assent, he turned hastily and beckoned to the young owner of the mill.

"Permit me, ladies—Herr Gerrald."

Traugott bowed with quiet dignity. The handsome man, proudly erect on his rearing steed, presented an attractive picture, at which Frau von Kartegg gazed with sparkling eyes.

Brand obstinately maintained his place at the side of the young baroness. Traugott had time only to exchange a few hasty words, then he was obliged to turn his horse and ride beside the opposite door.

Marie was flushed and embarrassed; the young mill-owner, too, seemed strangely agitated.

"I believe I have the honor of being your neighbor, *Fräulein*," he said, bending toward her. And Marie trembled at the sound of the deep tones, which hitherto she had heard only in her dreams.

"At least I am familiar with your name, Herr Gerrald," she answered, softly. "I liked to look at your house, it seemed so ancient and venerable."

Traugott could not turn his eyes from the embarrassed little face, whose large blue eyes were raised to his. It was the first time he had been so near her. Was she really beautiful? Her features were by no means regular, but delicate and full of feeling, and the expression of the eyes, the golden curls clustering around the temples, and the sweet girlish charm of her whole appearance rendered her irresistibly fascinating.

"Yes, our old house is interesting, is it not?" he asked, smiling. "Doctor Brand became very enthusiastic over the stone carving and the interior arrangement; he has discovered a quantity of treasures and marvels, which I should probably never have suspected. I mean curios, which require a taste for antiquities."

"And secret doors, cellars and corridors? Aunt Verja is always afraid when she visits us," replied Marie, in a jesting tone, with a mischievous side-glance, for his quiet manner restored her confidence. "We have an endless number of corners and nooks, too, till one reaches a bow-windowed room, and at night people who were afraid of ghosts would have a sad time with us."

"Aha! Then the rose-window in the upper story is your domain?" he said, slowly. "I think I often see you at the window, baroness."

"Mamma gave up the room to me," she answered, nodding, with a faint blush. "She has more space than she requires in the rest of the house, and I have arranged everything to please myself, collected all my treasures there, the roses and finches and—Ancestress Barbara."

"Marie, how long is it since the minister's wife went away?" interposed Verja, turning toward her. "You were speaking of it just now."

"Five days," replied the niece; and Frau von Kartegg again raised her eyes to the handsome horseman, who pleased her fancy. Then she turned to her *protégé* to give further instructions.

"Ancestress Barbara?" repeated Traugott, thoughtfully. "Is that the oil painting which hangs close by your window?"

Marie silently bent her head in assent.

"And you include that portrait among your treasures?"

What strange questions he could ask!

"Yes," the young girl confessed frankly, raising her eyes to his. "I am very, very fond of my pale ancestress. She has often been my only companion when I was alone and sorrowful; when no one else cared for me she always understood and—"

"That is why you took your friend from the gallery to the quiet bow-window room?"

There was a strangely set expression upon the young man's lips; he gazed at her with a fixed, earnest look.

"No," replied Marie, sorrowfully. "Mamma did not like the portrait, and because it had long been in the attic, she let it stay there, and was even unwilling to permit me to take it. This grieved me, so I cared doubly for it, and gradually learned to love the portrait. I was alone, like Barbara; so we suited each other."

"Do you know the history of that portrait?" He bent lower, and gazed intently into her eyes.

"Yes, I know Barbara Gerrald's story." A shadow crossed her face, and she tossed her head almost defiantly. "I know it, and yet I love her. That is strange, isn't it, Herr Gerrald?" She gazed quietly at him; a faint flush tinged her cheeks, but her lips still smiled.

His face brightened, as if illumined by a sudden flood of sunshine, and he turned hastily to curb his horse, which, rearing, resisted his control.

"Ancestress Barbara will bless you for it—and that other, too," he added, hesitatingly, grasping his bridle still more closely, "who loved her. What can I do for you, madam?"

"I asked you to come over to this side and answer a few questions," repeated Verja, gayly. "Don't you see you are on the verge of falling into the ditch, Herr Gerrald? Jonas, keep in the middle of the road."

Traugott glanced aside. Yes, his horse was barely a hand's breadth from the ditch; he would have plunged into it at the next bend of the road. The instantaneous consciousness of awkwardness which he felt as a skillful rider, and Brand's peculiar smile, sent the blood to his cheeks. He let the carriage pass, turned his horse, and crossed to the side of the beautiful baroness, who received him with a gay jest.

"Incredible!" she cried merrily. "What an interesting conversation you must have been carrying on to make you forget the gulf at your side; or was it the perfume of the spring blossoms? By the way, Marie, you are losing your rose."

Doctor Brand laughed more loudly than usual,

and murmured a courteous: "Charming!" while Traugott gazed gravely down at the little lady.

"It is true that I have the misfortune of being disconcerted by any unexpected incident," answered Gerrald, trying to smile. "Besides, I am really a great lover of flowers, and it is pardonable if one does become a little confused by unexpectedly finding such rare blossoms by the roadside. And then, I have had so little opportunity of meeting ladies of late that the pleasant accident might well embarrass me."

His features had grown still graver, and Verja's jesting mood vanished under the mournful glance which met her eyes.

"I heard of your loss, last year, with sincere regret," she answered sympathizingly, "and can understand your grief the better because only a few twelvemonths ago I stood beside my own mother's death-bed! My husband's self-sacrificing love made the wound heal more quickly, and the many proofs of friendship I received also contributed to divert my thoughts. Are you entirely alone in the world?"

"Entirely."

"Have you no relatives whom you could join?" Gerrald shook his head.

"No one in the whole wide world?"

Verja's heart quivered at the sound of his voice.

A sincere interest was awakened for this man, who was so handsome, so young and so desolate.

"You live entirely aloof from society, I have heard," she continued. "Have you no friends to whom you could express your feelings?"

"No," he answered sadly. "I have learned to despise society. Brand was the only person who sought me, and to him alone I owe this happy hour, madam."

Verja looked at him kindly. His sincere manner pleased her, perhaps on account of its rarity.

"Doctor Brand intends to enter society here," she answered. "He has promised to call on me; but since you hate the world," she added, mischievously, "I cannot possibly hope ever to welcome you to our circle."

"Oh, madam," he exclaimed, a deep flush crimsoning his brow, "I hate the world only to honor individuals the more sincerely. Would you permit me to accompany my friend?"

"You will always be a welcome guest, Herr Gerrald," replied the baroness, with a gracious bend of the head. "Unfortunately, the court-mourning prohibits any large entertainments, but it has issued no edict against friendly visits."

She raised her fan to protect herself against the sun, which was sending its golden beams into her smiling face.

Marie had heard every word and fancied that her heart must stand still in her delight. A swift glance sought Gerrald; he met it and smiled. Then her attention was again claimed by Doctor Brand, who was giving a very interesting description of the development of spring blossoms, and sometimes interweaving a little comparison to its resemblance to the dawning of love in the human heart.

Meanwhile the fleecy white clouds floated high above in the spring heavens, and the wooded hills rose on both sides of the road. Everything was calm and still save that through the green foliage echoed the notes of a song:

> "A youth saw a rosebud blooming,
> A rosebud on the moor."

CHAPTER VIII.

IN THE SNARE.

Pluto was taking his daily exercise, moving at an easy trot down the highway toward the mills.

On arriving, Doctor Brand flung the reins to a groom and ran up the stone steps. Gerrald, hat in hand, met him at the door.

"Shall I interrupt you?" he asked hastily. "I have come only for a few minutes."

"By no means, my dear friend," replied Traugott, courteously, taking his arm. "You've come just in time to be my guest. It will be a pleasant change to dine in your society."

"Oh, no," protested Brand. "I won't interrupt your noon rest. I am here merely to make an inquiry."

"We'll talk about that later," replied Traugott. "It would be a fine thing if I let you go after a three-minute visit. Perhaps, however, a Lucullian banquet awaits you, in which case, of course, my simple meal must retire into the background."

"Oh, no, no," said Brand, with a courteous bow. "I shall lose nothing at home, and should consider myself fortunate in accepting your invitation in preference to any other, but—"

"Then pray let us have no 'buts' and no compliments. You know that you are welcome, and as a friend, you certainly ought to go in and out of my house without ceremony."

He drew back to let the doctor enter, and after a little more hesitation the latter accepted.

The young mill-owner's room was very tastefully and comfortably furnished.

"Your little den is delightful," said Brand, turning to Gerrald, who was drawing the curtain to shut out the sunlight that glided inquisitively over the carved writing-desk and cast a shimmering glow upon the velvet covering of the sofa. "But, tell me, my dear Gerrald, don't you sometimes feel rather dull in this lonely hermitage?"

"Oh, yes," Traugott quietly assented. "It is often very melancholy, more sorrowful than you can imagine. Especially when, as I sit alone and desolate, a thousand memories of the past arise, and in the silence and gloom it is impossible to banish sad thoughts." Taking a pistol from the wall, he handed it to the visitor: "Look, this is an old weapon which will interest you. I inherited it from my grandfather. And to think that we are using similar firearms now!"

Brand gazed admiringly at the old-fashioned pistol and examined the ancient lock.

"But really, my dear friend, I must say frankly that I don't understand why you live so completely secluded from the world," he remarked carelessly, snapping the trigger up and down. "Under these circumstances, it really wouldn't be at all surprising if you should become a thorough hypochondriac. The period of your mourning is over, and although I don't blame you in the least for avoiding gay society and keeping out of it as much as possible; indeed, I can understand your feeling perfectly, still I think it is not healthful to carry the matter too far. An overdose of medicine produces an effect just opposite to what is desired; so let me for once be your physician and cure you of all these gloomy fancies. You know that I comprehend your feelings and mean honestly and sincerely by you; so trust yourself confidently to my care, my dear Gerrald, and rest assured that I will always give you the right dose."

Traugott, sighing, held out his hand to him.

"I thank you for your good will, Brand," he answered sadly, "but I shall probably be compelled to follow alone the path which I have now entered. I have found two effective remedies for old wounds, physical and mental exertion. They afford the only balm for such ails."

"Followed by rest and a little recreation," Brand remarked, with strong emphasis, suppressing the sarcastic smile which hovered around his lips.

Traugott interrupted the conversation by inviting Brand to dinner, which had just been announced.

Conversation between the two men was very animated, and the champagne had no little share in rousing Traugott from his cheerless mood; so, when the host and guest sat comfortably together over a cup of coffee, puffing clouds of smoke into the air, Doctor Brand could pursue his plan of campaign.

Knocking the ashes thoughtfully from the end of his cigar, he drew a carved mouth-piece from its case:

"I think it would be a good idea to go to the *casino* and drink a glass of beer! The heat is abominable for the lovely month of May, which, this year, seems to be a perfect parody on Heine. Do you feel no longing for Hebe?"

"If that is all," replied Traugott, smiling, "we

need not leave here. I'll give you my word of honor that my old wine cellar is still very respectably stocked, and that you will find good liquor in the ancient merchant-house."

Brand smoothed his mustache.

"I didn't doubt that an instant, my good friend," he said, with a graceful gesture of acknowledgment; "the whole house is planned for a good cellar; and I always say: 'Wherever the Lord puts a cellar he rolls the casks into it.' The ancestral Gerralds seemed to me to have been no laymen in the chapter of natural history concerning the noble fruit of the vine. Well, you are their worthy son. But, we'll reserve this pleasure for another day. Let us seek a few old acquaintances now and refresh ourselves with a glass of porter."

"To be frank, I feel no inclination to meet old acquaintances. It is uncomfortable to see them, after having avoided their society so long."

"But, for heaven's sake, my dear Gerrald," cried his companion, "do you mean to play hermit forever? I appreciate your determination not to return to the old mode of life, and you know my opinion of it; but I don't think you ought to shut yourself out of society entirely. There are too many evil tongues who might interpret it in a disadvantageous way, now that there is no excuse on account of your mourning, and your credit might be injured."

Traugott gazed at the speaker with a troubled expression:

"Impossible. How could—"

"You do not yet know the world, my young friend!" interrupted Brand, with a smile of superiority. "A young hot-head like yourself judges a picture solely by its colors. What you have hitherto seen of society consisted merely of illusions—masks, which dazzled by vivid contrasts. I have looked behind the scenes a long time, and found many a ragged bit of tinsel which, with the proper light, produced an admirable effect; but, when the lamps were screwed down and by accident the bright sunshine streamed in, the spell vanished, and all the impish faces appeared through the glitter. D—— is the focus of all sorts of gossip, and a young man like yourself, who stimulates curiosity and has attracted attention, turn and twist as he will, is, and always will be, the trial block on which everybody feels bound to inscribe something. Believe me, my dear Gerrald, that I mean honestly by you, and can judge of your position the better because I hear on all sides the most inconsiderate and varied opinions, and, therefore, formed my plan on them. That your sudden disappearance was attributed to every possible and impossible motive and led to the wildest rumors, is a fact probably not unknown to yourself!"

A slight frown darkened Traugott's brow.

"Worthy folk," he answered, not without a touch of resentment, "what atrocities will they not associate with my insignificant self? I believe that, were my back twice as broad, it could not bear the burden of all the enigmas connected with my every movement."

"Yes, you have really become a perfect enigma," answered Doctor Brand, laughing; "and if you had a hundred more sides to show, each would be represented as a Janus head with two faces. Well, don't worry about it, but trust entirely to me. I'll act for you, as a friend should, and see that Dame Gossip will soon lack material for any fresh fairy tales."

"I thank you, Brand," said Traugott, earnestly. "I am in a very uncomfortable position, and you are right. Turn and twist as I may, I can no longer justify myself to any one."

CHAPTER IX.

A CONFIDENTIAL CHAT.

Night had closed in earlier than usual, and while yesterday at this hour people had sat at their windows reading and working, to-day lamps were already placed on many a table, and looks of vexation were raised to the dark, starless sky ere the curtains were lowered.

Heloise was leaning against her window, softly humming a popular dance tune, and occasionally amusing herself by having her shaggy Bolognese lap-dog bring her the little satin slipper she skillfully tossed into the air, and, when a whine from Molly announced that she was hit by it, the dancer laughed merrily and flung her a biscuit, a payment which needed to be very frequently repeated.

"I don't want a light; take it away!" she said, curtly, without vouchsafing the maid a single glance. "Here, take Molly, too; the creature's eternal whining is insufferable. I'll get an Ulm mastiff; at least it will have a better voice." She picked up the animal as she spoke, gave its cold nose a farewell pat, and flung it somewhat roughly into Susanne's apron. The girl vanished with a pleasant nod. "This Brand is a terrible rake!" murmured Heloise, impatiently. "I've been waiting an hour already, and that's certainly a delightful occupation." She took a few hasty steps across the *boudoir*, and her attention was attracted by two notes which she had tossed carelessly on the table. Now *ennui* awakened her curiosity. She mounted a chair to light the burner in the chandelier, and then opened the envelopes. This momentarily diverted her thoughts, and was certainly a bit of good fortune for Doctor Brand, who, wrapped in a dark cloak, was just ringing the door-bell.

"Mademoiselle!" Heloise was reading meanwhile, "permit me to ask a respectful question. Your conduct, of late, has been extremely extravagant and offensive to me, perhaps too harsh to be attributed to mere caprice. You know that my regard for you is too deep for me to endure all these whims and torments longer, and I earnestly beseech you either to treat me more kindly or to accept in these lines my last farewell.

"LOTHAR, PRINCE VON X."

The dancer laughed and flung the note back on the table, then she turned toward the door where Doctor Brand had just appeared. The poor man received a welcome by no means cordial, though he kissed her hand with unchanged tenderness.

"Why are you so late?" asked Heloise, almost rudely. "I expected you at seven o'clock."

"It was impossible, absolutely impossible, my queen!" he said apologetically, letting his slender figure drop into an arm-chair. "I have had a great deal to do, Heloise; and have accomplished a great deal also," he added significantly.

"What? Tell me about it!" she exclaimed hurriedly, drawing her chair closer. "Quick, is he the same man he used to be?"

"Dear me, *signora*," replied Brand, laughing, as he coolly drew off his gloves, "do you suppose things move at such a rapid rate? Every matter requires time, and at present I am very well satisfied to have progressed so far."

"How far?" she inquired, with sparkling eyes.

"It is a long story, which cannot be told in two words—or yes, it might be done, but, of course, in that case many interesting details would be lost! But first, my dear friend, let me ask if you haven't some warm drink, which will strengthen the nerves. It is horrible weather, and I'm chilled to the bone! A tremendous gale, driving showers of rain into one's face, and at times the contents of a gutter poured down one's back. Aha, what rose-colored note have you here? 'Lothar?' From the prince? Pardon me, I must glance through it. I don't see letters from royalty every day!" He took the perfumed missive from the table and read its contents. "These are fine doings, Heloise," he said angrily. "What induced you to offend the man in this way. Do you want to break off your intimacy with him?"

The dancer shrugged her shoulders indifferently.

"If he continues to write me such silly notes, I shall probably be compelled to do so," she said sharply, with a saucy toss of her little head. "Do you suppose I could laugh and joke with him when I felt no inclination to do so? *Mille diables!* No. If I only liked him the least little bit; but I can't take the slightest fancy to his negro face." She laughed gayly.

Brand's eyes followed her disapprovingly.

"Do you know that you will be very unwise to forfeit the prince's friendship?" he said, sternly. "I should think you would have every reason to treat him graciously, merely out of regard for your pecuniary interests. Lothar is rich, and by no means a niggard in his love affairs, as you must know by your own experience!" He fixed his eyes on the diamond cross, which was glittering upon her neck. "Has he made you many presents?"

Heloise unlocked the carved cupboard and brought out a bottle of wine.

"Oh, yes," she answered carelessly, "a whole handful of little trinkets! But now, please, tell me what you have accomplished, and don't bore me with questions about things in which you have no concern."

Brand half closed his eyes and leaned back with folded arms.

"You are mistaken, my child!" he said, sharply. "This matter interests me more than you may, perhaps, imagine. I beg you to show me your jewels."

The dancer shrugged her shoulders, angrily.

"Just to try my patience to the utmost," she said. "I don't understand, Max, how you can find pleasure in tormenting me so."

He raised her hands coaxingly to his lips.

"I won't detain you more than five minutes, little goddess! And these five minutes will be so interesting to me. Let me see whether the ornaments are worthy to adorn you, the most precious pearl."

The Chênois laughed. Then, with a pout, turned her back upon him and went to the next room, returning with a large casket, which she placed on the table, and unlocked with a key fastened to the gold chain she wore around her neck.

"Most of these things came from Lord Langbury," she said. "He made me more valuable gifts than the prince."

Brand arose. His greedy eyes dilated at the sight before him.

"Lord Langbury?" he repeated. "Such a Crœsus might well make presents."

Heloise carelessly threw back the lid and let the precious stones sparkle in the light. They were magnificent gems, set in the shape of a star, whose brilliancy made him involuntarily shield his eyes.

Heloise, with a smile, raised the diadem and placed it on her dark curls. The mirror reflected a queenly vision.

Doctor Brand silently took ornament after ornament to scan them with covetous eyes. He seemed to be scrutinizing them closely, and the calculation made in his nimble brain reached a large amount. The stones lay sparkling on the table, and cast vivid rays upon the white hand of the woman who was impatiently gathering them up to return to the case, as careless and indifferent to their beauty as though the shining gems were pebbles collected on the highway.

"Well?" she asked, mischievously, shutting the lid. "Was the exhibition worth the fee?"

"Gossip says that your ornaments are priceless," replied Brand, with a strange smile: "but I think they are a royal gift which deserve to adorn your beauty. Don't be ignoble, Heloise, and repay the prince's generous kindness with base ingratitude. I earnestly entreat you to send him a pleasant answer."

"We'll see," was the careless reply.

Brand turned to the table and held the bottle up to the light to examine the label.

"This is undoubtedly fiery," he said, with a smile of satisfaction. "I thought so. Chartreuse! By King Artus, Heloise, your cupboard must be remarkably well supplied! A short time ago you produced a capital Benedictine, and now almost daily a different variety. We'll hope that this"—he patted the corpulent bottle—"will prove a worthy successor. Where do you get your stock, if I may ask?"

"Drink and tell me your story!" replied Heloise, curtly. Then she placed a *liqueur* glass on the table before him, and took her seat on the comfortable lounge.

"Won't you bear me company?" he asked, with a side-glance at the single glass.

"No!" was the sullen reply.

"So you are eager for my story?" he went on, with cruel composure. "So much the better; you will listen politely." As he spoke he closed one eye, held the glass up to the light and took a sip with the air of a connoisseur. "Yes, our chances so far are brilliant," he began, leaning comfortably back in a corner. "At first it was, of course, somewhat hard work to approach the good fellow; he seemed fairly panoplied by his beloved work and love of industry. But I attacked him with weapons which even these virtue-mailed walls could not withstand, and having taken advantage of a few opportune moments, spoken a few words at the right time, I had the pleasure of seeing one barrier fall after another, and was finally clasped to his heart as a friend; the main point was to induce him to trust me. Since then my position has been secure. I often make him feel my superiority in a useful way, and endeavor to strengthen my hold in all directions, in order to have complete *carte blanche* and at last be able to influence him. It is a difficult task to manage him successfully—one must touch so many strings at once! His temperament is high-strung; he has a great deal of family pride; his nature is still comparatively uncorrupted, a fact which, with his past, amazed me; he is animated by the best intentions—and is in love."

"What? In love? With whom?" exclaimed Heloise. Two steps brought her directly in front of him, and fixing her flashing eyes on his pale face, she exclaimed: "And you tell me this now for the first time?"

"That I don't know," replied Brand. "Pshaw! What does it matter? Some insignificant beauty, whom he will forget as quickly as he admired her."

"No, the fancy must go deeper, if he forgot me for it," answered Heloise, proudly. "Never mind;

it's nothing to me. I no longer care for his love. I want only my revenge." She winked her long lashes rapidly and let her beautiful head sink back on the cushions. A covert glance wandered over her companion's features, but she read nothing save an expression of innocent satisfaction. "Well, what else?" she asked, folding her arms.

"As I said before, I have taken the utmost possible trouble," Brand continued, "spun my nets and threads so fine that the worthy fellow could not help being caught in them—shuffled the cards so cleverly, and heaped so much combustible material that he could not help taking fire."

"And the result of all these efforts?" she interrupted impatiently, in a half-sneering tone.

"Will come in due time, my worshiped one. You see that I am proceeding in a business-like fashion with my report. Always go slowly. We ought not to expect too much from him at once, or stretch the cords too closely, else they might snap. I shall gradually bring matters to the point which will secure your revenge."

"Excuse one question, Max," said the Chênois, suddenly, in a thoughtful tone. "How does it happen that you are so extremely interested in this matter? It is not only your love for me. You are far too clever to act solely from the dictates of the heart. The brain must also have a large share in it, or your zeal would not go so far. Have you, too, a score to settle with him?"

"I? Oh, not at all! You interest me, Heloise. I feel an active sympathy in your love affair," he answered, smiling, "and am extremely glad to be of service to you in any way. Gerrald attracted my notice at the gaming table in Wiesbaden. He was a strange gambler. The rest you shall know at the right time, Heloise. For the present be satisfied with the assurance that it is of some importance to me also to have Gerrald pursue his old career. These are purely personal concerns which, in the first place, would not interest you, and of which, for the sake of a friend, I must not speak."

Heloise turned abruptly away.

"You are a fiend, Max. In Gerrald's case you deserve praise, but so far as you and your secrets are concerned, the deepest blame. There! Now go. The clock has just struck ten, and in spite of your pleasant society I have grown weary. So farewell, and good luck!"

With these words she glided past him as nimbly as an eel, and the next instant had vanished through a side-door, whose key turned in the lock.

A muttered oath followed her. Brand rose, angrily drained his glass, then lifted his gloves from the chair and went to her writing-desk. Several bank-notes and a small sum of money in gold lay in

The Opposite House. 89

a glass dish. He took two of the bills and slipped them into his pocket.

"I've borrowed some spending money, Heloise," he called through the keyhole. "I'm dead broke."

He received no answer and left the room.

He was soon standing outside in the storm and darkness. The rain beat into his face, the wind tore at his cloak, and the flickering street-lamp cast his shadow in long black outlines on the wet pavement as he glided noiselessly along in the shadow of the houses like a gloomy spectre of the night.

CHAPTER X.

YELLOWED PAPERS.

The general's widow, Frau Albertine von Rotterswyl, was sitting as usual in her comfortable armchair near the window. A piece of sewing lay folded in her work-basket, and her open book seemed to have been angrily pushed aside. Was it the fault of a tiresome chapter, or was there an unusual number of things to be seen in the quiet street? The old lady raised her head again and gazed impatiently down at the uneven pavement.

The baroness was one of those persons on whom the consciousness of belonging to a noble race is indelibly impressed.

Tall and slender, nature had given her the bearing which, in a parvenu, easily becomes stiff and affected, but invested her with a dignity whose haughty reserve appeared to weave a magic spell that uttered an imperious "Back!" to all who could not submit an escutcheon and coronet to the scrutiny of those cold gray eyes.

Albertine von Rotterswyl had two stepbrothers. The elder, Verja's husband, sometimes called as he drove by in a light carriage. The younger belonged to a regiment of the Guards in Berlin, and had been her favorite from childhood. Franz von Kartegg was a strikingly handsome man, daring and chivalrous, with velvety dark eyes, about which "whole books might be written," as a young lady had enthusiastically exclaimed. He had gone to the war in 1866, full of life and vigor, to return enfeebled and crippled by wounds. He was obliged to spend the greater portion of the year in Wiesbaden, and it was a heart-rending spectacle to see him, helpless as a child, in his rolling-chair.

Albertine had often cherished the desire to meet him again, but lacked the strength bestowed by the sudden power of "must," to rouse her from the fetters of her monotonous life. Now he was near her at Wiesbaden, and the baroness seemed to be planning a visit in earnest. She was slowly turning the pages of a railway-guide, estimating, and at times casting a searching glance into the street. Just at that moment the *portière* was drawn aside, and the servant put his gray head into the room.

"Frau von Kartegg and Doctor Brand!" he announced, and, at a gesture of assent from his mistress, he went back to usher the visitors through the long suite of apartments to the baroness's drawing-room. Frau von Rotterswyl rose slowly and greeted the newcomers with a slight bend of the head.

"I am glad that Doctor Brand has accompanied you, Verja!" she said curtly, inviting them, by a wave of the hand, to be seated. "I have long desired to make your acquaintance, Herr Brand. I noticed you as you rode by."

The gentleman bowed respectfully. The old lady's singularly abrupt manner somewhat confused him.

"If I had suspected, baroness, that I should be permitted to call, I would have done myself the honor of paying a visit here earlier. I have had the good fortune of making your daughter's acquaintance."

"I know it," replied the baroness, her keen eyes resting searchingly upon the pallid features of her companion. Then she turned to Verja. "Wouldn't you like to go up to Marie's room? She would be delighted to have a visit from you."

The young wife's white brow was contracted by a slight frown.

"There will be time for that afterward," she said; "but if you wish—"

"Yes, I do wish it," repeated Baroness von Rotterswyl, calmly; and Verja, rising, left the room.

Outside the door she paused, indignantly, to consider what she should do. Listen? No, she was too proud for that, so she must submit. She set her little feet on the floor more heavily than usual, cast a few wrathful glances at the closed door, and then rushed up the stairs, fairly trembling with excitement and curiosity. "You will wonder why I sent my sister-in-law away," said Baroness von Rotterswyl, smiling, secretly amused by the expression of astonishment on Doctor Brand's face; "but I have something to discuss with you which affects no one except myself, and to which I do not desire to give any publicity. Verja is a lovely woman, but she is gay and talkative."

Brand moved uneasily in his chair; the penetrating expression of her gray eyes embarrassed him.

"I shall be extremely happy to serve you in any way, baroness. You can rely on my discretion."

Frau von Rotterswyl's smile was peculiar, and the lines around her mouth and eyes were by no means pleasing.

"You are a lawyer, and therefore versed in legal affairs?"

Brand listened intently.

"I am no longer practicing my profession," he answered, eagerly; "yet I hope I may be able to aid you by my advice."

"Unfortunately, I fear that the case is too old to be opened," the baroness continued, with a courteous bow; "but it is better to do too much than too little."

She rose and walked slowly through the room. Brand watched her tall figure as she moved with a firm, steady step.

He, too, had risen, and leaned expectantly on the back of the carved chair, intensely interested, he could not deny; but, though he seemed extremely calm, the slight quiver of his nostrils, the distrustful glance which scanned every surrounding object, revealed the feverish excitement with which he awaited further developments.

The baroness returned with a few papers; the green curtain at the casement, stirred by the wind, cast a deep shadow over her features.

"Here are some papers," she began, in a tone utterly devoid of expression, "written by the steward of the Von A—— family. The whole drama took place on a friend's estate. Apparently the story has very little connection with me, yet it ruined my whole life. The entire affair will seem to you incredible, yet I have proofs—if necessary, witnesses. Read!"

Brand eagerly seized the package and read the contents, bending far over the table, while the paper rustled strangely in his hands, and by degrees every tinge of color vanished from his face till he grew as pale as death. It was not noticeable, for he was never ruddy, but his lips were almost livid, and the baroness's eyes rested, with a strangely penetrating expression, upon his features as, with her hand resting lightly on the table, she gazed at his bowed head. Suddenly, with a still keener look, she scrutinized his hair. There were white threads in it, and the roots had a reddish hue—*it was dyed!*

Brand did not see the baroness smile.

"Interesting—an unusually attractive case!" he exclaimed, straightening himself. "Unfortunately, the whole meaning cannot be understood. Perhaps you would have the kindness, madam—"

"This is the story," the baroness interrupted, almost harshly. "While I was maid of honor at the court, I visited at Castle H—— a friend whom I had known from my earliest childhood, both the lady and her brother Lewin. She was a widow, young, rich, beautiful and clever, and had spent the previous winter in Stuttgart, where she formed the acquaintance of a young count, who soon became a constant guest at her house, and in the summer accompanied her to H—— as her betrothed husband. She was infinitely happy, for she *loved* him."

Baroness von Rotterswyl paused a moment.

Brand leaned heavily on the chair.

"The count was a swindler," the speaker continued. "One day he disappeared with more than half of Ida's fortune, and Lewin was found dead in the forest."

"And was no trace of the murderer discovered?" exclaimed Brand, excitedly. His voice sounded hoarse and unnatural. "How could that be possible, madam? Did you not denounce him at once?"

"In vain. Not the faintest clue was ever obtained. Count Berndt had disappeared. My friend grieved herself to death. She was attacked by nervous fever and died. Her last words were the name of the man whom she had so ardently loved. It was she who, on her death-bed, forbade any further search."

"And now, after so many years, would you wish—" asked Doctor Brand, with an incredulous smile. "I think, after so long an interval, the sharper must have effaced every trace."

"Certainly," replied the baroness, nodding assent. "But look—this account recalled the whole affair to my memory."

She took a newspaper clipping from the table and handed it to him. Doctor Brand hurriedly seized the scrap and looked at the marked portion.

"A Remarkably Artful Speculation," was the heading of the article, which described in detail a robbery in W——, where the swindler had met with an exasperating degree of success. Obtaining admittance under a false name to a wealthy family, he had won the affections of a young lady, in order to steal jewels and papers of considerable value.

"Ah," said Brand, drawing a long breath, "that is certainly singular. The same story I have just read in these documents. You are quite right, baroness, to come forward, too, and renew your accusation. Perhaps the criminal will prove to be one and the same person."

"That is my idea also," replied Albertine, quietly, her searching eyes scanning Brand's features. "It would be interesting to learn whether justice still exists in the world. I myself believe that my case has long been outlawed, and would not take any steps until I obtained the advice of an expert. My sister-in-law has told me so much of you and your obliging disposition that I thought of applying to you, and hope you will pardon my request."

"I shall consider myself fortunate to act for you in any way, baroness. Perhaps you wish me to make inquiries at once?"

"Oh, no," said Baroness von Rotterswyl, "you must take no special trouble on my account; but if you would simply have the kindness to keep the matter in view, I should be grateful."

"Certainly, madam." Brand bowed courteously, with his habitual smile. "I shall know how to value your confidence. Should you need me, no matter when or where, I shall always be at your service."

"I thank you for your kindness, Herr Brand. I see that my sister-in-law has not told me too much of your readiness to oblige. Then, for the present, may I ask you to notice the reports which may appear. As a young man of the world, you can do this far better than an old woman like me in my solitude. Perhaps you will call occasionally to let me know the result. You will always be a welcome guest here."

Brand raised the slender fingers of the baroness to his lips and courteously thanked her.

"I shall spend much of my time near you, and await any sign, madam. My friend, Gerrald, has the valuable quality of being your neighbor, so I shall have the best opportunity of frequently passing your door."

"Do you know Herr Gerrald?" asked the baroness, with marked coldness. "True, I remember that Verja mentioned it; he is a merchant, isn't he?" The old lady drew herself up to her full height, her lips curled slightly. "He has made himself the subject of considerable gossip, fragments of which I have heard. With whom does he associate here?"

"He is to attend the *musicale* given by the minister's wife, day after to-morrow," said Brand, with a somewhat malicious expression.

"What?" cried the old lady, starting up. "At the minister's?"

Brand bowed assent.

"Good heavens!" The baroness paused, and pressed her cambric handkerchief to her lips. "I shall be interested in hearing your account of the young man's appearance there. I suppose you are invited too, doctor?"

"I shall go with my friend," replied Brand, rising to offer a chair to Frau von Kartegg, who had just entered, "and will bring you a report of everything, madam. I hope to please you in both cases."

Verja and her companion had gone; but the baroness still stood in the center of the room, with her figure drawn to its full height, and her eyes fixed on the door behind whose *portière* his black figure had vanished. There was a peculiar expression in her gray eyes, a look of mingled hate and satisfaction, an almost uncanny sparkle, which threatened to burst at any moment into a blaze. The baroness, drawing a long breath, laid her slender hand upon her heart and raised her eyes toward heaven. Then she took the yellow papers and carried them back to the secretary, in whose secret drawer lay various mementoes, a withered bough from an oak-tree, crumbling after the lapse of years, and a small pen-and-ink sketch. The old lady raised it almost reverently and bent low over the faded lines. It represented a very handsome man, haughty and full of life, with slightly waving hair and sparkling eyes. Many a tear seemed to have fallen on the paper; the name below was scarcely legible—" Lewin."

Marie entered. The baroness shut the drawer and walked rapidly toward her.

"My daughter!" The trembling girl had never heard her speak in so gentle a tone. "Do you love me, Marie?"

Her mother had never addressed her in such a way before. Scarcely trusting her own ears, the young girl threw herself into her arms.

"Mamma!" she faltered. "My dear mamma!"

Then an unprecedented thing happened—the baroness bent toward the rosy little face and imprinted a kiss upon the beautiful brow, tenderly stroked the fair hair, and said:

"Be very joyous to-day, my little Marie; laugh and sing and be happy. It is a great festival for your mother!"

CHAPTER XI.

TABLEAUX.

The room at the right of the wide hall had been fitted up by her excellency, the ambassadress, as a stage. The broad folding-doors were removed, and in their place hung a purple curtain. Cloth draperies of the same hue covered the walls on both sides, shining with a subdued glow in the light of the countless gas-jets. The rays flashed from chandeliers and candelabra, and were reflected a thousand-fold in the bronze-framed mirrors. The long suite of apartments was also radiant with light as far as the richly furnished dining-room and the corridors, which skillful hands had converted into veritable arcades of blossoms. Fragrant flowering plants filled the niches and corners, laurel and oleander in graceful groups surrounded the white marble statues, and delicate vines were twined around the pillars of the ball-room and drawn in garlands to the ceiling.

Silken trains were already rustling over the floor, glittering uniforms mingled with the elegant costumes of the ladies; the stars and ribbons of various orders vying with the sparkle of the diamonds and pearls which this evening adorned fair necks even more lavishly than usual.

The band, concealed behind tall groups of plants, was already beginning to play, and the hostess, a stately woman in a very effective costume, was passing through the groups of guests, with a pleasant word for each. Now she hastened to the first row of arm-chairs, directly in front of the stage, placed for the older guests, seated herself beside one of the ladies, and soon became engaged in an animated conversation. The person thus distinguished had chosen a somewhat isolated seat. Her tall, erect figure was attired in black moire antique, and her jewels were magnificent pearls. The old Baroness von Rotterswyl was a rare guest, and her appearance in her excellency's drawing-room had awakened the utmost astonishment. People could not understand it, and made one conjecture after another to account for the remarkable event.

The curtain was drawn slightly aside, and a head covered with dark curls appeared before the brilliant throng. Then it vanished, and a slender figure the next instant bowed before her excellency.

"Welcome, my dear Frau von Kartegg," exclaimed the hostess, with a rapid glance of admiration at the young matron. "I am delighted to see you here. There are doubtless many crinkles to be smoothed behind the curtain."

"Everything is going on admirably, your excellency," replied the Russian, gayly. "Our performers are all here, and we only await the arrival of the principal guests to begin."

"The duchess will be punctual," said the hostess, with winning cordiality. "The poor little stage-manager has a great deal of responsibility on her beautiful shoulders this evening, and were it not for our Verja, who regulates everything, I should almost be anxious."

Nodding cordially, she left the young wife to several gentlemen who wished to offer their homage, and also their dancing cards, at Frau von Kartegg's feet.

"There is a spark under all the ashes," whispered Brand, with a long glance at the baroness. He and Gerrald had obtained a corner near the stage. "That woman has marvelous taste in dress. I believe if she were gowned in gray sackcloth she would still outshine all her gayly clad sisters."

Traugott's eyes rested admiringly upon the graceful figure standing in the center of the hall under the full blaze of the chandelier. Several gentlemen surrounded her, as shadows hover about light, and the charming woman had for each a jest or clever remark mischievously spoken.

A satin gown of the brightest golden yellow fitted her slender figure closely, and fell in shining folds in a long train, over which gold-colored crape floated like rising clouds, caught here and there by glowing scarlet flowers, diffusing a heavy fragrance, or a glittering cluster of feathers which, against the golden background, looked like tongues of flame. Her dark hair curled gracefully around her forehead, below the diadem, of which no princess need have been ashamed; locks of shining dark hair fell low on her neck, interwoven with sprays of scarlet flowers.

Verja dropped her fan and turned her beautiful head. Her gaze wandered around the room, to rest at last with a look of satisfaction on Gerrald's tall figure. With a gracious farewell to the group of attendant cavaliers, she stood the next instant before the tall, fair-haired man, who bowed low and deferentially to the radiant vision.

"Why are you so apart from the rest?" she whispered, with sparkling eyes, permitting her *protégé*, Brand, to raise her slender hand to his lips. "You seem to have arrived late. Have you been presented, or met any acquaintances?"

"We have paid our respects to her excellency," replied Traugott, in a somewhat unsteady voice, his eyes wandering to the group of young ladies. " Unfortunately, I have not yet had an opportunity to approach the ladies. I suppose Fräulein von Rotterswyl is not in the room ?"

Verja smiled.

" She has vanished behind the scenes. But tell me, Herr Gerrald—you look unusually pale to-night —do you want to make yourself interesting, and work mischief with those melancholy eyes?"

She shook her finger mischievously at him.

Gerrald really did look weary and haggard; his eyes seemed more deeply set than usual, and a shadow rested on his brow.

" I have had a great deal to do, baroness," he answered, forcing a smile. " I attend to every detail myself."

" Even cut my own coupons," added Brand, in a jesting tone. " It 's hard work !"

" You have a provoking tongue, my worthy sir," retorted the Russian, laughing. " I can easily imagine that you would be Herr Gerrald's right-hand man in such matters. By the way, have you been presented to Frau von Rotterswyl?"

Traugott started.

" Oh, no !" he stammered in embarrassment. " I don't even know whether I can venture—"

" Certainly you can," replied Verja, nodding pleasantly. " I will present you myself."

"And I?" asked Brand, with languishing eyes.

"If you behave prettily, we'll take you, too," replied Verja, gayly, turning hastily toward the door. "Ah, here are our sovereigns. Farewell, gentlemen. There is old Prince George, too. *Au revoir!*" As she spoke she glided swiftly through the crowd and vanished behind the curtain.

Traugott leaned against the pedestal of a Cupid taking aim, and pressed his hand upon his heart. The tempest raging in his soul filled him with embarrassment. He compelled himself to turn his mind to other thoughts. His eyes, unconsciously, wandered over the sea of heads to rest upon the figure of the duchess. Gerrald had seen her almost daily in the street, and was familiar with her features; yet, this evening she did not look the same. Her fair hair was very becoming to her fresh complexion, and her sea-green silk had been chosen to suit the Southern tint of her complexion. Prince George stood by her side, greeting the hostess in his usual cordial manner, while Baron von Kartegg, the hereditary prince's adjutant, had respectfully taken the old gentleman's tea-cup to carry it to the chair reserved for his royal highness. By degrees the movement ceased, the seats were filled, and all eyes rested upon the curtain, which must rise the next instant.

A bell rang. The hall was still as death. The

musicians softly began the air: "A Wanderer with Staff in Hand."

The curtain rolled up, and a low murmur of satisfaction ran through the audience. The lights had been turned down, and, amid the darkness, glowed the bright tableau of the wanderer in the arms of his gray-haired mother.

Loud applause rewarded the artists. Again the curtain rose, revealing a lonely, dusky convent garden, at whose right was a carved image of the Madonna, while, amid the many vines, knelt a pallid woman in the garb and veil of a nun.

"How beautiful the little English girl looks!" ran through the ranks of the spectators in a whisper. "She just suits the tableau."

Thus picture followed picture. A scene from the "Meistersinger." How superbly Herr von Esen personated *Hans Sachs*, and what a charming little *Eva* Bertha von Lenk made! *Undine* rose from the cool waves; *Mignon* alternately bewailed her sorrows and rattled her tambourine, and flames cast their vivid glare upon the picturesque camp of the gypsies. The tableaux swiftly succeeded one another, with constant variety.

Suddenly a servant moved rapidly through the crowd and requested Doctor Brand and his companion to follow him. Traugott thought that there must be some mistake; but there was no time for questions, and he silently obeyed. He was conducted through an ante-chamber to the stage, where Verja stood in an attitude of despair.

"Ah, there you are, Herr Gerrald!" she eagerly exclaimed, hastening toward him. "You savior in time of need! Just think—we have no *Faust!* I am frantic—fairly frantic!"

She pressed her hands wildly upon her throbbing temples.

Gerrald gazed at her in astonishment. He did not yet fully understand.

"Count Launers has left us in the lurch in the most inconsiderate manner," the Russian continued, excitedly. "He disappeared ten minutes ago, leaving this note. There, what good can that do me? And even if his friend lay at the point of death ten times over, half an hour—"

"Would not have permitted him to see him alive," interrupted Herr von Sallich, gravely. "Launers was obliged to leave at once—"

"And our *Faust?*" cried Verja, almost angrily.

"I hope Herr Gerrald will supply his place," said some one soothingly.

"Our tallest gentlemen have already tried on the costume, and it hung round them like a bag!" Verja went on, dejectedly. "You are our only hope, Herr Gerrald. Your figure is similar to the count's, and your appearance, too, would suit the character.

Pray have the kindness to help us out of our dilemma."

Traugott bowed, flushing to the very roots of his fair hair.

"If Fräulein von Rotterswyl is satisfied with the exchange, madam, I can only consider it a special honor to fill Count Launers's place. If you need me, I am entirely at your disposal."

"Then you will do it!" cried Verja, joyously, holding out both hands to him. "A thousand thanks in advance! Baron Sallich, please take Herr Gerrald to the gentlemen's dressing-room," she called to a young officer. "I have no more time now—not a moment, my dear Herr Gerrald," she added in her usual jesting tone, "but I shall hold my breath till the trial is over."

Traugott hastily followed his guide, who speedily obtained the *Faust* costume, and the gentlemen pressed forward eagerly to watch the young man as he began to put on the dress.

When he returned to the stage many an eye followed with admiring glances the haughty, erect figure which wore the black velvet doublet with almost royal dignity. Even Verja was surprised, and watched the tall form with an expression of delight.

True, Gerrald made a somewhat juvenile *Faust*, but his assumption of the character could not fail to interest by its originality.

"Splendid—splendid!" she cried. "We shall all fall in love with you, Herr Gerrald!" And again her eyes wandered over the handsome man from head to foot. "The costume fits as though it had been molded on you. Now I'll see if my *Gretchen* is ready. Here, look at the picture, meanwhile. That is your pose."

She vanished behind the scenes.

Gerrald stood with a throbbing heart, gazing at the picture in his hand. So she would cling to him in that way? He was to put his arm around her.

Closing the book, he paced hastily up and down the narrow space; the murmur of voices reached him from the hall, sometimes deadened by the music, sometimes rising above the softer passages; there was a pause in the tableaux.

Traugott was becoming more and more excited by the thought of everything awaiting him. He scarcely dared to believe that it was his own image reflected in the mirror, and that he stood awaiting the girl who, to him, was earth's rarest jewel. He moved nearer to the glass, threw the heavy cloak across his shoulder, pressed the cap with its floating plume lower on his brow and moved it up and down a little, then resumed his pacing to and fro, but more slowly, as though, by this monotonous motion, he hoped to soothe the tumultuous emotion which made his heart throb almost to bursting.

Then the curtain was drawn back, and Verja pushed *Gretchen* upon the stage.

"There are a few minutes yet. I'll come presently and arrange the tableau. Refreshments are being served to the audience."

Then she vanished, and the young girl stood alone before Traugott, confused and blushing. Gerrald involuntarily advanced a step toward her as she timidly raised her blue eyes to gaze in silent astonishment at the striking beauty of his appearance.

"Aunt Verja told me that you would take Count Launers's place, Herr Gerrald. I thank you for the kindness."

She uttered the few words timidly, almost in a whisper, and scarcely ventured to meet his radiant eyes.

"The kindness is to me, baroness," he answered, hastily. "Accept my heartfelt thanks. I can scarcely believe this sudden good fortune—cannot yet grasp the thought which seemed so unattainable and was so suddenly realized! Forgive me if I perhaps advance to your side too boldly—obey your aunt's summons too willingly!"

Marie looked up, smiling and happy.

At last the stage was set for *Martha's* garden.

"Isn't Doctor Brand ready yet?" Verja called back.

"Brand? Is he to appear in the tableau, too?" asked Gerrald, in surprise.

"Oh, I forgot—it was to be a surprise to you also. Of course. Brand is our *Mephistopheles*. Ah, there comes *Martha!*"

Gerrald turned, a hand was laid heavily on his shoulder, and, almost startling in its disagreeable resemblance, *Mephistopheles* laughed in his face.

"Capital!" said Verja, approvingly. "You are enough to frighten us. Go into the background at once. Do you see this picture? That's your position in promenading with *Martha*. Herr Gerrald and Marie, come here, please; close to the front."

It was not difficult to group the handsome couple advantageously. Gerrald could easily fix an admiring glance upon Marie's face; clasp her slender figure tenderly. True, he scarcely ventured to touch her, and the first time Verja was obliged to say: "Don't be too stiff, Herr Gerrald." The second attempt was much better.

At last everything was ready. *Gretchen*, with face averted, counted the white petals of the daisy. *Mephistopheles* and his companion were in the background.

The curtain slowly rose, a soft melody from "Faust" greeted the exquisite picture. There was no other sound in the hall; the audience scarcely ventured to breathe. *Gretchen* trembled in the embrace of the handsome man. She dared not raise her dark lashes, and fancied he must hear the rapid beating of her heart, which threatened to stifle her. The folds of purple cloth fell, a death-like silence still reigned, broken by thunders of applause, shouts of encore—till the enraptured audience again beheld the tableau, which was the masterpiece of the entertainment.

Marie involuntarily leaned closer to the handsome man; her eyes questioned the white petals a second time. "He loves me—loves me not—loves me not."

Gerrald looked marvelously well. The noble head, with its regular profile, seemed chiseled from stone; the haughty features were motionless, and, as he took his position the second time, the cap had slipped back and his thick fair hair fell low over his white brow—the accident enhanced the beauty of the tableau.

"Who is it? Who are they?" was asked on all sides. A tumult of voices rose, and, like a cry of victory, the names "Rotterswyl," "Gerrald" echoed through the hall.

Two eyes alone rested with a fixed, lustreless gaze upon the beautiful picture, two hands were convulsively clinched in rage among the folds of black moire antique. They were the hands of the widowed Baroness von Rotterswyl. A sudden tempest of wrath raged in her soul, her wounded pride rebelled against the name which blended with hers as if it were a matter of course, yet which ought to remain for ever as alien as the fire which is quenched when it meets with water.

Meanwhile the curtain, in response to the insistent applause, rose for the third time. *Faust* clasped his *Gretchen* proudly in his embrace, and, as the curtain slowly fell, he whispered, softly:

"What did the flower say, baroness?"

Marie, with quivering lips, silently shook her head; but his glance met eyes which, with divine innocence, confessed: "I love you."

No one noticed it save one diabolical face peering through the branches of an oleander, above which nodded the cock's plumes in a pointed hat—*Mephistopheles!*

* * * * * *

One mild spring evening in Wiesbaden two men met each other in the Kurhaus grounds and exchanged cordial greetings.

"Now tell your story, brother of my heart," said one. "By all the imps of the nether world, Brand, you are a marvelously clever fellow, and if I did not feel your warm hand in my fingers, I might believe that you were the Old Nick in person! Pardon the compliment, it's meant in all kindness. So you are here! Zounds, it has been quickly done! And Gerrald, too, I hope, with the bank bills."

"If you would lower your tones one-half, I could hear just as well," replied Doctor Brand, with a shade of indignation. "Remember that we are not alone." His eyes wandered over the open space behind the Kurhaus, between whose pillars the guests were moving to and fro; then, thrusting his arm through his companion's, he led him into the shaded grounds. "Of course I have him here; the whole clan, in fact," he went on, in a lowered tone. "But what does that avail? Many a drop of water will flow down the Rhine before we get him to the gaming-table; the fellow is more obstinate than ever. The virtuous baroness abhors gamblers, and I fear that will be enough to make the lover refuse to touch a rake again. Deuce take the whole feminine sex!"

"That would be a pity," said his companion, "when we don't bow under her gentle yoke—"

"I hope, Otto, you will be fireproof," interrupted Brand, with a hasty side-glance. "Pshaw, I know you love the fragrance of flowers—everybody to his taste—but I think our night-moth doesn't stick long."

Herr Wikke paused, and relieved his feelings by a tolerably loud laugh.

"You seem to have turned hypochondriac in

D——, Hans," he cried, slapping his friend on the shoulder. "I think such an idea would be rather insulting to a fellow of my profession. And what is to become of our plans? They are nearer to my heart than the whole fair sex." He stroked his red mustache as he spoke, and his little, twinkling eyes wandered over the open portion of the grounds. "I have but *one* sweetheart in this world—gold—gold with its shining little face. It's the fortune of war. One person cuts another's throat, and I believe everybody will soon pray: 'The Lord preserve us from our friends.' Gerrald is still intimate with you?"

Doctor Brand quietly twisted his glossy mustache.

"It would be better to put it the other way. I have honored him with little of my confidence, and when I have enjoined secrecy, the tales I told him usually existed only in my imagination. I have imparted various harmless matters, spoken earnestly and penitently of former youthful errors, and wasted many words where I desired to use but few; life only too frequently hinges upon trifles. Hitherto I have had brilliant success; how matters will continue—we shall see!"

"Brains like yours, Max, devise ways and means daily," said his companion, nodding thoughtfully. "Since you have been successful thus far, we shall finally carry our point. How is the little Chênois?"

"I didn't find her at home the last time I called, but sent her a farewell note," replied Brand, absently switching the dusty leaves from the bough with his cane. "It wouldn't be a bad thing for us to have the pretty Heloise here. True, she can't help much, but she has often suggested clever ideas, and, which is the main thing, she would be a prize for our table. Her jewels are not to be despised. True, she has no vacation now—it's the wrong time. But at all events I'll write to her. Who knows? Heloise is a little witch. She has accomplished far more than a few weeks' leave of absence."

"But our venture—what of that? It's infamous that we are compelled to change places."

"Everything is ready," whispered the other mysteriously. "We have found two capital rooms in the second story of a house in G Street. They are in the rear, look out into a secluded garden, and have two ways of egress. The lower floor is occupied by a small restaurant, whose landlord has joined us. The man is an old acquaintance of Luckardt, and we can trust him implicitly.

"Whenever you have time, call for me. I'll take you there. Luckardt will get a new folding roulette table. I'll obtain the three broken rakes from Frankfort. That's all that is necessary. Have you talked with Luckardt?"

"Not yet," replied Brand. "I have been here

scarcely forty-eight hours, and this is the second time I have left the house. So we are now to carry on the business upon a somewhat grander scale."

"At any rate we must first whet Gerrald's appetite at the Kurhaus. Then he will afterward prefer to play secretly on account of the baroness, and, when the lion has once tasted blood, I should like to see the magician who can restrain a passion like that of the handsome Prince of the Mills! Ha! ha! ha!"

"And are you still of the opinion that we must sail westward?"

"When we have enough—unquestionably," replied Brand, with an unpleasant degree of confidence. "Do you imagine I will remain here longer under the noses of the police?"

"And Heloise, what will become of her?" asked Wikke, with a sensation of some slight discomfort.

"Heloise? She'll soon dance the lost ducats together. A few evenings, a new admirer, and her gems will be replaced. *She* is my least anxiety. She is pretty, clever, and can also be very entertaining. Besides, in case of necessity she will make some wealthy suitor happy with her hand."

Wikke made no reply. Both turned into the nearest side-path. Before them lay the little lake, whose mirror-like surface extended in the rear of the Kurhaus. Brand followed it with a certain appearance of haste.

The trees on the shore hung their leafy boughs low over the water, and at the left two small islands rose abruptly from the surface, one densely wooded, and washed by the waves, the larger one connected with the shore by a bridge. Dainty gondolas, with gay streamers and canopies, moved to and fro over the rippling waves, pausing ever and anon in a shaded cove, or, steered by a lady's hand, floating in the center of the lake.

It was indeed an animated scene as the sun shone so brightly down upon it, casting golden spots upon the white plumage of the swans; countless ducklings and coots were gathered on the shore, diving, swimming, and trustfully emerging on the velvet turf whenever some child's generous hand scattered crumbs of bread.

Two ladies, both tall and slender, whose figures bore a marked resemblance to each other, were standing beside the railing opposite the Kurhaus.

Doctor Brand involuntarily stopped and pressed his companion's arm more closely.

"The Von Rotterswyls!" he whispered hastily. "Good heavens, that's the last thing I expected. Come, Wikke, turn down this path. I'll go home with you another time; you see that I must speak to the ladies—it is necessary to keep on good terms!

I can't introduce you; neither your name nor your looks are suitable to present to such eyes. *Addio!* I'll look you up to-morrow." Then he hastened on, and in a few minutes was standing before Baroness von Rotterswyl, who welcomed him with evident pleasure.

Wikke shaded his eyes a moment with his hand, and gazed in the direction of the group, then turned obediently and strolled leisurely through the leafy avenue of Wilhelmstrasse.

Otto Wikke was one of those persons whom we meet by hundreds at the present day—a broken-down genius, whose talents, under better guidance, even if they had won no distinguished place, would have secured their possessor a position in which he might have been useful to society. He had been educated, but on account of a debt of honor was compelled to leave the university, and thus had ruined his life.

So he came by accident to Wiesbaden. He had two florins in his pocket—whence obtained he had long ceased to ask. But he went to the green table, staked them, and won four in exchange. Again he staked and won. He continued to play, still winning, and whether Dame Fortune had invested the two dirty coins with some sweet spell or Samiel had held them fast on *rouge*, Wikke won more than two hundred florins.

The passion of gambling seized his very soul. His eyes dilated at the sight of the sum of money constantly growing under his hands; he gathered the clinking coins with greedy fingers; his insatiate eyes, glittering with excitement, rested on the luck-giving *rouge*.

Just at that moment a hand, heavy and cold, was laid on his shoulder.

"Stop!" a voice hissed into his ear, and a pair of fiendish eyes glared down at him. "The luck is changing."

Wikke started, and gazed with an almost idiotic expression into the face, ghostlike in its pallor, of this monitor, then almost mechanically drew back his money and arose.

"Come with me!" whispered the stranger, smiling pleasantly. "You are a favorite of fortune. I congratulate you, but you are gambling for the first time—far too eagerly, and that will lead to no good end." So he took Wikke away to a room where champagne was sparkling, and a well-furnished table offered an inviting supper. Then Wikke, with a giddy brain, went up to his miserable attic room. He had found a new career, a future which unrolled itself in the most radiant hues, and a friend, who called himself Doctor Brand.

So he had remained in Wiesbaden, daily took his place at the green table, and sank from step to step, till he at last stood at the sharp turn from which there are only two paths. Either the way leads to that dark portal whose iron grating closes behind the criminal for life or it ends at the gulf whose farther shore is called "America," a gulf so wide that ninety-nine out of every hundred sink ere they set foot on the land.

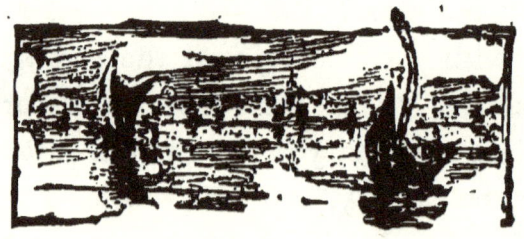

CHAPTER XII.

ON THE SPOT.

The train was rushing through the scorching sunshine, two shining rows of rails glittered under the wheels and vanished in serpentine curves among the dry mounds of sand. Here and there a solitary fir tree or a clump of brown junipers stood beside the road; with that exception the whole region was desolate. Beyond Frankfort the scene changed. The blue outlines of mountains rose against the sky, the waves of the broad Main and Rhine glittered, and dark pine woods cast their pointed shadows on the yellow sand.

Heloise had left D—— suddenly, ostensibly for a month. She had complained recently of pains in her limbs, said that she positively could not dance any more, and the physician had willingly given her a certificate which at once secured leave of absence from the court stage.

She was now travelling directly to Wiesbaden, and, in her *ennui*, wondering what she should find there to amuse her. She did not wish to gamble.

There was only one lady in the carriage—an elegant, aristocratic woman, with sparkling eyes and a Southern complexion. Her leather bag had the initials " V. von K.," surmounted by a coronet. Heloise recognized her as the admired darling of D—— society. She herself had often peeped through the curtain concealing the stage and envied the beautiful Madam von Kartegg her seat beside the princess. She knew that Brand and Gerrald visited her, and she determined not to leave this opportunity of making her acquaintance unused. A Frenchwoman possesses natural grace of manner, and when Heloise chose, and did not lapse into her off-hand air, she could vie with any fashionable dame.

"Pardon me, madam, but does the closed window annoy you?" she began, in perfect French. "The carriage is so terribly close, it would be better to open it."

Verja, too, was weary of solitude; she spoke French well, liked to use the language, and was glad to find entertainment. Conversation followed.

The dancer had opened the window, and then resumed her seat, smoothing the folds of her rustling silk. She looked extremely pretty under the thin gauze veil.

"Where are you going?" asked Frau von Kartegg, in a tone of interest. "But, of course, it must be to the springs. Who would pass them at this season?"

"To be sure, madam," replied the Parisian, smiling pleasantly. "I expect to use the waters at Wiesbaden and, to be frank, anticipate much pleasure from the change. Nothing is so detestable to me as *ennui*."

This touched the most responsive chord in Verja's soul. She eagerly assented, and they were soon chatting as gayly as old acquaintances.

The young matron felt singularly attracted by the unusually piquant manner of her companion. Her conversation was light and amusing—a swift play upon words, such as only Frenchwomen can manage, who use many thousand words without really saying much, laugh and jest, yet never bore one with the light froth of their talk.

Verja was pondering. Where had she seen those mischievous eyes? Where had the saucy little nose, with its delicate arch, charmed her? And where had those scarlet lips, that bright little soubrette face, attracted her attention? She knew that she had seen them somewhere.

"It is possible that we may meet in Wiesbaden," she said, kindly, "and in that case I should like to know what name to give you, *fräulein*. Shall we exchange cards?"

She held out a dainty bit of pasteboard.

"'Verja, Baroness von Kartegg,'" Heloise read; then turned to the Russian, with a winning air of surprise. "A very familiar name to me, baroness. Who has not heard of the star of our drawing-rooms? It is accident, not presumption, which led me to make your acquaintance. I am Heloise Chênois."

Like a flash of lightning Verja's memory returned. She now knew where the little face had bewitched her. *Satanella!* Pride and curiosity struggled for an instant in her heart, but the latter conquered.

"Mademoiselle Chênois?" she exclaimed, in a jesting tone. "And you did not tell me so long ago, but quietly let me grope about in the darkness, when the light was so close at hand, you *artiste par excellence?* I am extremely glad to make your acquaintance, *fräulein.*"

Verja's enthusiastic temperament instantly kindled into eager admiration of this entertaining companion. How much she had heard of this woman! The romantic episode with Gerrald was enough to awaken a desire to know its heroine. She would have been glad to question Heloise about him and request an explanation of many things, but the fear of being indiscreet restrained her. And Brand? What had he not told her concerning the endless variety of Heloise's whims and caprices?

So those were the lips Gerrald had ardently kissed; those were the glowing eyes which gave the sentence of life and death; that was the bewitching smile which turned the heads of men! And this dainty, elegant creature in silk and lace was the leading ballet dancer, the queen of the stage, the sovereign of the day, and—the deserted lady-love of the handsome Prince of the Mill! Was it not interesting? Verja could not weary of asking questions about the romantic side of the mimic life behind the footlights. Her new acquaintance understood how to describe it entertainingly.

An hour in a railway carriage often makes people better acquainted than a year of formal social intercourse; and the mutual interest felt by these two vivacious women was very great.

A shrill whistle interrupted their conversation. Verja seized her sunshade and straightened the little straw hat resting on her waving hair. The Frenchwoman buttoned her light-gray gloves and looked out of the window.

"Wiesbaden!" she nodded. "How quickly the time has passed!"

A noisy throng was surging to and fro upon the platform.

"Marie!" called Verja from the carriage, and the young girl rushed to the door, exclaiming with delight:

"Have you arrived at last, dearest aunt!"

"It is fortunate, child, that you have come to receive a poor grass-widow with military assistance," said Verja, laughing and giving her a tender embrace. "So much the better. Now I shall have courage to make my way through this human deluge. Adieu, mademoiselle. I hope we shall meet again," Verja called back, and the next instant vanished in the throng.

"Who is that lady?" asked Marie. "She is very pretty."

"Mademoiselle Chênois," said Verja, hurriedly.

Heloise also sprang from the carriage. It was some time before the trunks could be found, and she was so impatient to get away. At last she was seated in the carriage, rolling down sunny Wilhelmstrasse.

The Kurhaus gleamed in the distance. There were the gaming-tables. There she would see Gerrald again.

"Good luck," she murmured, laughing. "Now let the drama begin. I shall be on the spot."

CHAPTER XIII.

A CRISIS.

A motley throng crowded the halls of the Kurhaus in Wiesbaden; gay melodies, in whose alluring waltz-measures the very heart and soul melted, were heard. A full-dress ball was being given in there.

A large party of acquaintances had just returned from a promenade through the illuminated garden. The merry group assembled in a side-hall to consult what should next be done.

"Suppose," said Doctor Brand, "that we walk through the gaming-halls as swiftly as fate and as noiselessly as the wind, and watch the players at *trente et quarante?* We shall risk neither colds nor baths, and not stray too far from the fountain of champagne."

"Bravo, so we will!" answered several laughing

voices. A young officer offered Verja his arm and moved toward the gaming-halls.

"I shall not join the party," said Gerrald, with a clouded brow. "Go with Fräulein von Rotterswyl, Brand!"

"Don't make yourself ridiculous," the latter hissed into his ear. "Do you want to waken old memories and gossip by such extraordinary conduct? People will ask, 'Why doesn't he come?' and receive the answer: 'He distrusts himself!'"

This had its effect. Gerrald bit his lips and offered Marie his arm. A tempest was raging in his soul, and the young girl noticed his agitation.

"Shall we stay behind?" she asked softly.

A deep flush crimsoned his face, and he raised his fair head proudly.

"Certainly not; why should we?" he answered almost roughly, and passed through the open door.

"I hate gambling and its devotees!" said Marie, with an anxious glance at his pale face. A strange feeling stole over her, a dread which fairly stopped her breath.

Gerrald smiled faintly, as he replied:

"So do I."

A foreboding haunted the young girl. She wanted to ask him to turn back, and began to address him in a grave, earnest tone; but ere she could finish her sentence Brand turned and put his finger on his lips. No talking was allowed in the gaming-hall.

They were standing beside the roulette table.

"*Rouge!*" cried the croupier's monotonous voice. "*Trente et un!*" and hands pocketed the coin with trembling haste, the ball buzzed and hummed as it ran down; and the unvarying voice continued its call, while the gamblers listened with feverish excitement. Ah, when the ball stopped it sent a thrill through nerve and bone.

"Let us go!" whispered Gerrald. "Let us move on!" He passed his hand across his brow, and his restless eyes wandered to Marie. A gold band glittered in her hair—gold, wherever he looked.

He pressed forward to another table. The croupier held a pack of cards in his hand.

"*Faites votre jeu,* messieurs!" he said, as he slowly turned the cards. Again that strange thrill ran through Gerrald's frame. How often he had stood at that table, betting with feverish excitement on that game. How often the cards had turned in his favor; how often they had gathered up his gold—forever. He stood gazing fixedly at the gay bits of pasteboard, his lips parted, and a feverish flush glowed on his cheeks.

"Won!" he cried with sparkling eyes.

The sudden exclamation made Marie look up; the expression of his face startled her.

"Let us go, Herr Gerrald!" she timidly entreated.

"Go!" he repeated, as though in a dream. "Yes, let us go," and went silently back to the ball-room, where the band was beginning to play.

Marie stood still and pressed her hand upon his arm.

"I don't like that frown on your forehead, Herr Gerrald!" she exclaimed, and then added, beseechingly: "Promise me not to go back there!"

Traugott passed his hand slowly across his brow.

"Fear nothing," he said, with a strangely fixed expression, "it will smooth again."

They danced together. Then Marie was claimed by a young *attaché*.

"Let us drink a glass of wine. Come, my friend." Doctor Brand put his arm through Gerrald's and drew him away.

The wine glowed like fire in his veins, and his brow became deeply flushed. Brand constantly refilled his glass.

"Have you been watching the play?" he asked.

"Yes; at two tables."

"And did you feel no desire to try your luck?"

The tempter bent close to him, smiling.

Traugott laughed.

"No; I dare not."

"Are you a slave? Who rules you?"

"My conscience."

"Don't be a simpleton, Gerrald, and drop such follies, which may suit prudish spinsters, but not a man. Put on petticoats and sit in a corner, if you haven't courage and strength enough to govern your own passions. If you don't wish to play, very well; omit it, but at least go with me. I want to risk something to-day."

Gerrald ground his teeth as he started up, and hurriedly advanced toward him.

"Never dare to sneer at me again, Brand, or you shall learn to know the man whom you would like to put into petticoats! Come, I'll go and show you whether I have a will of my own or not."

Gerrald followed him to the *trente et quarante* table and, leaning on Brand's chair, gazed steadily at the white hand of the croupier, which so calmly dealt out life and death.

He glanced up hurriedly as Brand held out a handful of coins.

"Won!" he said.

Then, as his dull gaze roved over the long table, he started as he met a pair of sparkling eyes. At the end of the table sat the gold-witch, in an exquisite toilet, and resting her head, with its crown of dark curls, on her hand, smiled at him—Heloise.

Traugott gazed into those dark eyes as if spellbound. Was not that the same sweet, alluring smile with which she had charmed him, which he had idolized and then abandoned? All the blissful visions of former happiness rose before his memory; he was compelled to think of the hours which he had dreamed away in her society; he saw the fascinating creature dance over the boards; heard her gay laugh when she pledged him from the foaming goblet.

The sounds echoed around him as they had done in those days; the green cloth wavered before his eyes, and notes of sweet music floated faintly from the distant ball-room.

"Will you bet with me, Gerrald?" asked Brand, holding out the gold coin. "Try once."

Traugott took it; it burned between his fingers and intoxicated his senses; he no longer realized where he was, what he had promised; he knew only that everything around affected him like a spell; he mechanically held out his hand—and staked it.

Brand rose, and Traugott, dropping into the chair, unconsciously took the heap of gold which he had won. He played on and on; the sum increased under his hands, and the passion of gambling glowed in his eyes and crimsoned his brow with a deepening flush. Curious spectators gathered around and watched him. He was not aware of his own good fortune.

Bank-notes came to him, but he pushed them

heedlessly aside. He wanted to see nothing but gold —*gold!* He reveled with increasing pleasure in the wealth, and made the coins clink against one another.

"Stop!" Brand whispered. "You have a large sum there."

Traugott staggered to his feet.

"What dance is beginning now?" he suddenly asked an acquaintance, hastily fastening the coat which he had thrown back while playing.

"The third," and the young man hastened on.

"I must go," exclaimed Gerrald. "Stay here, Brand. I'll be back soon."

He hurried to the ball-room without looking back, and therefore did not see Doctor Brand approach the "gold witch," and slip something into her hand. She was evidently delighted, and questioned him, but at a wave of his hand she concealed the gold case in the folds of her dress.

Marie was standing near a pillar in the spacious hall, glancing sadly over the throng seeking *him*.

Traugott hurriedly approached. His face was flushed, and his hair hung in tangled locks about his pale face.

"Pardon me," he said, in an agitated tone, "I did not know that the dance had begun."

"Where were you?" asked Marie, her heart beating passionately as she raised her eyes with a beseeching, anxious look, as if she dreaded his reply.

"Over yonder," he answered, excitedly. "I could not help it. The sounds were so alluring that I was forced to play. Have you ever heard the coins ring till the echo reached the inmost depths of your soul? The wine was so fiery that it went to my head. But I have won—won an immense amount of gold."

Marie's sweet face grew deadly pale as, pressing her hand upon her heart to stifle a sharp pang, she struggled for composure.

"Pardon me," continued Traugott, in an agitated tone. "Do you hear? That is *Il Bacio*. Let us waltz."

"Back!" she answered in a trembling voice. "Do not dare to touch my hand."

He looked fixedly at her with a questioning gaze. He did no understand her meaning.

"I told you just now my opinion of gambling and gamblers, Herr Gerrald," she said, her breath coming more quickly as she drew her slender figure to its full height. "I hate frivolous people, men who break their promises. I do not comprehend the changeable mortals who cannot keep their word, and will have nothing to do with those for whom my request has so little value."

She had put out her hand to thrust him back, and her eyes rested on him coldly and calmly. All the pride of her nature rose in rebellion in her heart, rending between her and her lover a chasm whose yawning black depths threatened to swallow her whole happiness.

"Good heavens!" he exclaimed, almost vehemently. "Are these words meant for me?"

"They are my farewell to you, Herr Gerrald," she answered, faintly. Her hands were clasped, and her blue eyes filled with tears. "Forget me, as I, too, will forget that I have ever known you."

"Marie!" he cried in horror. "In the name of Heaven's pity, stay!"

But the young girl did not hear. She had turned and did not see the terrible change in his features as he struck his brow with his clenched hand and stood gazing after her like a somnambulist. She moved steadily on, and a voice in his heart seemed to utter a cry of despair.

"What is it, Gerrald?" asked a low voice behind him. The voice which had lured him to destruction.

"What is it?" replied Traugott, with blazing eyes. "A settlement with you, Brand!" He approached him with clinched hands, his voice hoarse from emotion.

"Don't be a fool!" said the other, laughing. "Do you want to quarrel with a friend because a haughty girl has at last found a pretext for giving you your walking ticket? Ha, ha, ha! Do you really believe that a Von Rotterswyl bade you farewell because you once staked something on cards out of *ennui?* Nonsense! If she loved you, she would have forgiven you after giving a kindly warning to respect her wishes. The fair baroness is tired of her plebeian toy and now flings it into a corner. She availed herself of the first excuse, and she was compelled to tell you plainly because you, innocent fellow, did not notice that your attentions were becoming wearisome."

Traugott had blanched to the hue of marble, the veins on his forehead swelled, and a scarlet flush crimsoned his cheeks for an instant.

"Have mercy, Brand," he groaned.

"Mercy? In order to say a few sweet words about yonder amiable young lady?" Brand jeered rudely. "Don't be a Braekenburg, to bewail an insolent beauty! Are you not your own master? How did the little girl have the presumption to prescribe rules for your actions? Come, Gerrald, raise the flag of defiance and show that the rich Prince of the Mill can live without a baroness. Come, my friend, now we'll be jolly. *Vive la joie!*"

Traugott laughed. The sound was terrible. Even Brand shrank.

"Be jolly, be jolly!" he repeated, with wandering eyes. "You are right; we will be gay! At the green table sits a woman, reckless, beautiful—and with no coronet. It is long since I have kissed any lips. I yearn to humble myself to the dust. Come, Brand, I will try whether a ballet-dancer can forgive!" He rushed through the long suite of apartments and leaned over Heloise's chair. "Do you love me still, Heloise?"

She started up, shaking her curls back from her brow.

"Gerrald," she whispered, "have you come at last?" And clinging to his arm with beaming eyes, she drew him toward the open door. "Come, dearest; the lanterns are swaying outside, the moon is shining on the quiet lake, and the green branches will repeat no tender whispers."

Marie walked silently beside her uncle Franz. Her head had sunk on his shoulder, and she wept burning tears. All this misery had come upon her so quickly, so suddenly; the sweet dream was forever shattered. A single quarter of an hour had decided her earthly existence. How could she help breaking down?

A little island in the lake was connected with the land by a wooden bridge. Tall trees shaded it, and the slender branches of glimmering alders dipped into the water. To this spot Franz von Kartegg led his grieving niece.

Marie suddenly started and stood as though spellbound. Surely, those loud, passionate tones were

Gerrald's. It was he standing there in the bright moonlight. And the woman before him, sitting so carelessly on the bench, with her hands clasped around her knee—was not that Heloise?

A pang of bitter anguish pierced the heart of the young baroness. Her pure soul rebelled. She longed to make her escape, yet could not help pleading with heart-rending sorrow:

"Stay, uncle; I must see whether he has entirely forgotten me."

"Heloise!" cried Gerrald, with vehement passion, "do not upbraid me for a love which I neither will nor can deny. You charmed me as a woman rarely has power to do; you fettered my soul and held to my lips the sweet potion which makes a man forget the world; you rendered me joyous and happy by your love. But you never filled my heart with that blissful consciousness of purity bestowed by that other woman, whom I loved with my whole soul, and whom I can never forget, though Brand were right a thousand times over in saying that she trifled with me—that she never loved me. Marie uplifted me, opened a new life before me, and when the waves again surged around, striving to drag me down to the abyss of ruin, she pitilessly let me sink. I once deserted you, Heloise, because I was struggling upward to a height which I was never to attain. I wrenched my passion for you from my heart because I thought myself too good for such a love; and now I return, pleading once more for this forfeited happiness in the dust before you. Can you deny me?"

He had knelt on one knee, and with his handsome head bowed awaited her reply. And Heloise bent toward him, but the glance fixed upon him was that of an adder, and the voice sounded cold and heartless as it hissed in reply:

"Once! Do you remind me of those days, Gerrald? Very well, then; I, too, will recall the past to you. You wounded me to the very depths of my soul, scorned me, trampled my love under foot; but I swore a terrible oath that I would have my revenge upon you for that hour! At that time *I* knelt before *you*. I also pleaded for pity; you might have saved me, rescued me from the boards of the stage, but you heartlessly thrust me back, condemning the dancer to the dust of the world, while you were to soar upward, high into the radiant ether, where such wretched worms as I need no longer be seen. Fool that you were! You held before my eyes a talisman, saying: 'This arms me against you!' And I swore by the salvation of my soul that you should atone for those words, if there were any such thing as justice in the world. You should lie in the dust before *me*, as I did then before *you;* you should sue for the love you disdained, as a dying man pleads for life. That hour has now come, and I, too, hold my talisman before your eyes. Do you know this, Gerrald?" She raised her hand with savage exultation; the moonlight shone upon a dull gold case and a rose-wood cross. "Do you know it, Gerrald? The white flower which your *Gretchen* probably wore in her hair? Without this blossom you will be a miserable, perjured man. And now rejoice, demon of vengeance—now I condemn you!"

Traugott had started up, with a sudden cry of alarm, but she had already flung the jewel far out into the lake. The water dashed upward, then all was still.

"Now look for it, my friend!" she said, with a scornful laugh. "I am avenged, and my mission is accomplished. Give your love to your baroness. I now stand before you for the last time. You treated me harshly, inflicted bitter pain, but my dagger deals incurable wounds. Live on, and remember me!"

Slipping past him with the speed of thought, she rushed back along the path, flitting noiselessly through the moonlight in her glittering dress like a spirit of evil.

Traugott stood rigid and motionless as a statue. A soft hand was laid on his shoulder, and he looked up with a startled glance.

"Marie!" fell in tremulous accents from his lips. "Marie?"

She stood before him in her pure, bright beauty, her eyes resting gently, yet mournfully, on his face.

"Traugott!" she said, softly; and the young man, as if utterly crushed, sank down on the bench, covered his face with his hands and groaned aloud.

The words she addressed to him were earnest and touching; they fell like refreshing dew upon his darkened soul; but he did not once look up at her until she paused. Then, raising his pale face, he murmured:

"I am superstitious. That flower is lying deep in the lake, and I cannot be happy without it. But I will seek for my white blossom, though I should descend into a watery grave."

He rose slowly, but Marie anxiously stepped before him and, in an agony of dread, threw her arms around his neck.

"No, I will not let you go to that flower!"

Gerrald bent his head and gazed with joyful comprehension into her tearful eyes.

"Do you love me, then, Marie?"

"Yes, I love you, Traugott," she whispered, in half-stifled tones, "and therefore I must guard your life, that you may not destroy it with a blasphemous hand. Your mother took your legacy from you, because you were no longer worthy of it, but she left open to you the path which leads upward through expiation to the grave. If it is Heaven's will that you should die, it will send to your heart the bullet destined, not for the criminal, but the defender of Germany. France has declared war. Serve your native land, and if the wrath of God demands your life, at least yield it on the field of honor."

"Marie," said Traugott, softly pressing her hand to his lips, " may Heaven bless you for these words! You have restored me the hope, the consolation of at least dying an honorable death, and if I offer my breast to the enemy's artillery, there will surely be a compassionate bullet which will grant a guiltless grave to the perjured—"

Tears were streaming down Marie's cheeks, as she leaned her head on his breast and bade him farewell. It was a sorrowful betrothal, and a still sadder parting. She clasped her lover's hands in benediction, but Traugott pressed his lips on her pure brow, and bade her an eternal farewell.

Meanwhile, tumultuous excitement pervaded the halls of the Kurhaus—the dispatch, which brought the news of the declaration of war by France as a terrible fact, was being read aloud.

CHAPTER XIV.

BY LAW OF MIGHT

Doctor Brand must have had some unpleasant experience. He was hurrying, with a very gloomy expression, through the streets in the direction of Heloise's lodgings. On arriving he rushed up the stairs, and did not even consider it necessary to wait to be announced, but barely pausing to knock, entered.

Heloise raised her head and looked at him in astonishment. She was kneeling on the floor before her trunk, rummaging among the heap of articles which Susanne had piled around her; closets and drawers, partly cleared of their contents, stood open.

The dancer threw down her embroidered negligee jacket and let her hands rest a moment.

"*Mon Dieu!* Brand, how long has it been the custom to bounce in after this fashion?"

The visitor did not answer immediately; he was

gazing with an angry frown at this chaos of boxes and bundles, and ended by giving the tall wicker trunk a contemptuous kick.

"What does all this mean, Heloise, if I may ask?"

The dancer folded her arms defiantly, and gazed at him with a contemptuous shrug of the shoulders.

"How long have you controlled my plans, if *I* may ask? I should think you might request information courteously, instead of putting your questions with German bluntness. You are not addressing one of your minions."

Brand stamped angrily on the floor.

"So you mean to leave here," he said, grinding his teeth. "Perhaps I may have a word or two to say about it. But first tell me what happened to Gerrald yesterday? I must suppose that you parted in anger."

"In anger? Oh, no, with all possible ceremony and courtesy!" she answered, in a mocking tone, without looking up from her work. "Poor Gerrald scraped his knee sore before me, and raved about the past; then I ventured to refresh his memory a little, and told him a short, delightful story about those old times, and, being now a thorough gourmand, I tasted his heart's blood drop by drop. When I took leave, I dealt a death-blow. We were once such good friends, so I rendered a friendly service. I took care that the ugly gold case should no longer weigh upon his heart, and flung it into the lake near the Kurhaus. So you see that I have no further interest in Gerrald. I am avenged, and this ends our compact, old friend. Your other plans have little to do with me. I would have helped you willingly had I known them, but it is too late now. You see for yourself that our paths separate from this day."

"Separate?" cried Brand, in a terrible voice, his eyes fairly devouring her slender figure, leaning so lightly against the table, its graceful outlines scarcely concealed by the folds of thin muslin. "Remember your promise, 'Pledge for pledge.' Now I demand my payment, comrade!"

Heloise had turned pale. She involuntarily drew back a step and clasped her hands.

"The times have changed," she said proudly, half averting her head, so that her delicate profile stood forth in strong relief against the window. "I am a Frenchwoman, you are a German; our nations have declared war against each other, and should I trade with an enemy of my own nation? Never! Here, Brand, take these gems; they are a royal reward for the service you have rendered me." She unclasped the bracelet from her pink wrist and held out the glittering ornament.

Brand approached in great excitement.

"Do you really expect to buy my claim on you

with this miserable tinsel? Do you really believe that for this trash I would resign the hand promised to me? You are mine, Heloise, and woe betide us both if you do not keep your pledge!" Snatching the bracelet from her hand, he hurled it violently on the floor; his fingers clutched her rounded arm with an iron grasp, drawing her passionately to his breast; his hot breath fanned her cheek as he covered her lips with kisses.

"Brand!" she shrieked, struggling to release herself. "Hear me, Brand. I will offer much for my liberty. I do not love you, you monster, and I would make your life a very hell of torture, if you tried to bind me to your side. I should poison you with my breath, slay you with my kiss, drain your life like a vampire."

"You do not love me?" said Brand, coldly drawing back. His momentary intoxication had passed away, and his calculating mind warned him to avail himself of the favorable moment. "Well, then, I do not desire a wife who does not love me. But listen, Heloise. I am now no longer the man who, with ardent passion, sues for your love. I am the usurer who demands his compensation, and who will not leave the spot until he has the entire sum in his hands. What will you pay me for your torn note?"

He stationed himself at the bell-rope and, with

threatening arm, barred the way to the door. She saw that she was in his power, and the consciousness of her helplessness made her limbs tremble till she felt like a frightened child.

"Here—my necklace, my cross, ten thousand *thalers* in money—"

"Nothing more?" he asked, laughing.

"I have no more!" she groaned, wildly.

"Indeed! It is well to have a little information. For instance, where is the pretty casket in which the white stones sparkle? Show it to me again, my angel. I have a great desire to see them."

The dancer's hand clenched in terrible fury; she longed to rush upon the scoundrel and kill him; then a bright idea entered her head.

"Brand, I will be your wife."

"Really?" he asked, in a mocking tone, with a low bow. "You do me too much honor, my gracious lady. More than I can possibly accept after being favored with a rejection. So the diamonds, mademoiselle?"

Heloise saw no escape. She still stood hesitating. Despair seized upon her, but his mysterious eye warned her by its savage menace, and, tottering to the bureau, she brought out the costly ornaments. Placing the casket on the table, she raised the velvet-lined lid, scattering the gems over the mahogany top with reckless haste; and the sun shone through the window, making lightning flashes of color dart around her trembling fingers.

"Is this enough to buy a soul from Satan?" she asked, in an expressionless voice.

"It will do tolerably well," replied Brand, with a nod, as he let the gems slip separately through his fingers, and then flung them back into the casket. "One thing more, however, *ma belle*," he pleaded, with a mocking assumption of gallantry. "Might I ask for a little dedication? Here are pens and paper. I will dictate only a few words. Write, mademoiselle; I am in a hurry."

Heloise calmly took the pen—everything was now a matter of indifference to her—a fragment of her heart seemed to have been wrenched out with the gems.

Brand slowly repeated the form of words, and she wrote that she gave him the diamonds as property legally acquired by purchase. Then she added her name, and Brand even pressed her seal beneath it for security.

"Everything must be in due form," he said, derisively. Then he read the lines once more and folded the paper. "What do you intend to do now, my dearest?"

"I shall go back to my native land, and hope to return shortly with my victorious brothers to recover my jewels."

"Very hopeful!" he cried, laughing. "Well, I wish you good luck on the journey, as well as in everything else. We have been good friends so long, were even engaged to be married, so I hope we shall not soon forget each other. I have done my utmost to aid you to fulfill a wish, and think you will perceive that you ought to 'do as you are done by.' *Au revoir!*"

He took the casket under his arm and seized his hat. A low, sarcastic bow, and the door banged loudly behind him.

CHAPTER XV.

THE HOUR OF PARTING.

War had been declared. Bodies of troops were constantly passing through Wiesbaden. The peaceful watering-place resembled a camp, and patriotic enthusiasm had reached its height.

Traugott Gerrald willingly obeyed the order which summoned him to his regiment. He was to leave in the evening. The parting was difficult; but he now saw a goal—a lofty purpose in life for which he could struggle—a flood in whose waves he might drown his sorrows forever.

Marie von Rotterswyl had been greatly agitated by the news of Gerrald's departure. The confidant of her love affair, her uncle Franz, whose invalid condition would not permit him to take any share in the conflict with the enemy of his country, had brought the tidings. But Uncle Franz had again won her warmest gratitude. He had rowed out in a little boat on the Kurhaus lake, and at last succeeded, to Marie's intense delight, in finding the golden case—Gerrald's "talisman." It had caught among the water-plants, and he had thus been able to restore to Marie her lover's treasure.

"I must see him to give him back the case," the young girl entreated.

"Already? I would not do that until his return," said Franz.

"And suppose he should never return?" she exclaimed, gazing mournfully into his eyes. "No, uncle, he must take his talisman with him when he goes to the war. I have thought of everything, and if it is God's will, have chosen the right course. Where do you think I can see him?"

"There will be no time at the railway station," said Mr. Kartegg, thoughtfully. "The best plan would probably be for me to go to him. He just asked if he might see you once more. I dissuaded him on your mother's account. The poor woman is too excited to be able to control herself."

"But I can't take leave of him in the public street," said Marie.

"Yes, you are right there, my child. H'm! What if I should take you to the drawing-room in the hotel. If your uncle is with you, you can receive him without hesitation."

A few minutes later Marie was standing with a throbbing heart in the large drawing-room of the hotel, gazing around her at the long mirrors, which reflected her image so many times that she had unconsciously paused and pushed the waving hair back from her brow. A faint flush tinged her cheeks, and the black veil framed her face like gauze intended to relieve the dazzling hue of marble. The girlish figure in the black wool dress was very earnest and grave of aspect.

Hasty steps hurried through the ante-room. Marie started, pressing her hand upon her heart. He was coming—and now the door was pushed open and Traugott stood before her, breathless from his rapid walk.

"Marie!" he exclaimed, in a voice trembling with joy. "How I thank you for giving me an opportunity to say farewell!"

He held out both hands and gazed into her eyes with a look of radiant happiness.

"I could not let you go without a parting word," whispered the young girl with downcast eyes. "I struggled with myself a long time, but was forced to give you this last hour to soothe my heart and conscience."

"What a blessing this last hour will contain," he said, softly. "What a consolation it will bring during all the sorrowful ones which must yet be endured! Now that I know you have really forgiven me I can go forth to meet my fate with a lighter heart. Now the bullet which has chosen my breast for its goal will have no more terrors, and if I must die, it will be with the sweet consciousness that no living soul harbors resentment against me. Will you bear me in remembrance, Marie? Will you include me also in your prayers when you implore mercy for all who have sinned?"

An infinite anguish thrilled her; dread for the heart that loved her so tenderly. With a sudden impulse, she held out her hand and raised her tearful eyes to his.

"Yes, I will pray day and night!" she said, faintly. "Not for the dead. My petitions will be that God may guard the living man, for my sake!" Then, with a trembling hand, she drew from her pocket a small sealed package, tied with a white ribbon, on which were embroidered in blue silk the words: "God guard you." "There was another reason for my coming," she said, in an unsteady voice. "I have a new talisman, a memento for you, with the request that you will accept it from me. But before I give it to you, you must promise me something."

Gerrald looked at her inquiringly; a sorrowful expression hovered around his lips.

"It is granted," he said, in a low tone.

Marie hesitated a moment; her cheeks crimsoned and she seemed deeply embarrassed; then, raising her eyes with an earnest look, she said, solemnly:

"Promise not to break this seal, Traugott, unless it is God's will that you should be severely wounded, so severely that—that there would scarcely be a hope of recovery. Then you may break it—not before."

She had scarcely been able to utter the last words; her heart was beating so that it almost stifled her, and the thought of the possibility that he might open it with fingers stiffening in the death-chill almost made her senses fail. But she controlled herself. She knew that she ought not to make the parting hard for him, and, with a touching smile, held out her hand.

"I promise!" he said, earnestly, clasping it closely.

Then Marie fastened the ribbon round his neck, and he hid the memento in his breast, kissing the ribbon and the hand which bestowed it, while the young girl whispered, amid her tears:

"God guard you!"

CHAPTER XVI.

A BOTTLE OF TOKAY.

After Brand had gone and Heloise, wringing her hands, had convinced herself that the diamonds had actually vanished forever, bitterness and resentment raged with terrible fury in her heart against the tool by whose aid she had just satiated her vengeance on another. Pacing swiftly up and down the room like the incarnation of hate, she brooded over vengeance, and tried to devise plans for most swiftly and surely regaining her lost treasure.

Wild thoughts darted through her brain, nearly all fantastic and impracticable; one alone she did not reject, and pondered over the explanation. What was the secret between him and old Baroness von Rotterswyl? Wikke had given various vague hints that Brand was forced to be on the watch for spies; he had talked of a time in the past of which he did not like to think. What was the chapter in his life that he was forced to fear?

The dancer stamped impatiently on the floor.

She must get out of doors, and had already seized her lace shawl and sunshade to prepare to go into the open air, when some one knocked at the door, and, to her great astonishment, Wikke appeared on the threshold.

Heloise glanced angrily at him, but this melancholy-looking fellow could not possibly have heard of Brand's rascally trick, and the sorrowful glance with which he scanned the trunks and boxes had evidently not yet seen the flash of the diamonds, which his friend had doubtless carefully kept out of sight to turn into cash privately. This conciliated her, and put into her head a new idea, which she resolved to execute.

"Herr Wikke," she asked, approaching him, "how do I happen to have the honor of your visit with the mercury standing at eighty-six in the thermometer?"

"I've just met Brand," he answered in a troubled tone, "and learned from him that you were going away, mademoiselle. I couldn't believe it, and was obliged to convince myself in person whether the bad news could be trusted."

"That is very charming of you," said Heloise, kindly, "and I rejoice to be able to assure you that I shall, perhaps, remain several days longer. It depends entirely upon my own whim, and whether my friends make my stay here agreeable. But sit down, *mon ami*, and spend a few hours pleasantly with me. It is very warm to-day, and one needs refreshment."

She smiled most winningly and held out her hand. Wikke suddenly felt much warmer than he had outside in the sun, and protested, with almost blundering haste, that he should consider it an honor to bear his beautiful friend company. His time was entirely his own until eight o'clock; then, of course, he would be engaged.

Wikke had associated little with elegant women; with coquettish queens of the stage probably not at all; so the dancer's charming manner fascinated him the more as, with easy familiarity, she leaned near his chair, gazing at him with mischievous eyes.

Heloise could be bewitching when she chose, and now she exerted all her arts to bind her companion with the fetters in which even crowned heads had languished.

She had long since discovered that he was not one of the favored children of Intellect, but merely a cunning sharper, who knew his trade very well, but in the presence of this alluring woman was like a raw youth, scarcely able to move his limbs. She had noticed that Brand had said nothing about the diamonds, because their value would be greater if not divided, and she also knew that Wikke was familiar with the assessor's youthful experiences.

Her plan was matured. One friend should throw around the other's feet the snare which she only needed to draw to bring the victim into the trap. In the opposite cupboard stood a bottle with a slender neck. The dancer brought it to the table and let the sparkling drops flow into the glasses. It was Tokay, which makes the blood flow more swiftly through the veins.

Wikke was fond of good wine, though he could not bear much. Now, when Heloise pledged him, and he could drink from the same spot which her red lips had just touched, he raised the cup with twofold joy to drain it to the dregs.

Heloise had drawn the curtain aside; the crimson rays of the setting sun cast glittering reflections on her slender figure. Resting her head on her hand, she gazed steadily at him, constantly urging him to drink, and when he would not do so alone she touched glasses with him.

"Brand has just been here," she said; "but I am very angry with him, and he is the sole cause of my departure. Did he tell you nothing about it?"

"Not one single word!" protested Wikke, passing his handkerchief several times across his brow. "You are angry with him, mademoiselle; may I ask why?"

The Frenchwoman sipped a little wine from her glass, then carelessly raised it and pledged him.

"Why shouldn't I tell you? It was about a

Madam von Rotterswyl. You probably know nothing concerning the matter."

"Rotterswyl?" interrupted Wikke, with a stupid glance. "Oho, what about it?"

"He told me that he had known her, had made the acquaintance in a very unpleasant way. But drink another glass, Herr Wikke, I have more wine in the cupboard."

"Unpleasant? Ha, ha, ha!" laughed her companion, with a cunning twinkle in his eyes. "Does he consider such things unpleasant? Unpleasant! Ha, ha, ha!—and did he tell you nothing more?"

"He put me off till another time, when he would tell me the whole story," said the Frenchwoman, with a keen glance at his glassy eyes. "But no, I don't want 'another time,' and I shall stick to my determination to leave to-morrow."

"Ha, ha, ha! Don't do that, my angel!" said Wikke, with a loud laugh. "There's a tale connected with the old witch; but it's a confoundedly ticklish business, and whether I can venture to speak of it—"

"Well? Wasn't I right in thinking that you are not a whit better than your friend Brand?" cried Heloise, with feigned indignation. "I'll ring for my maid at once, that my trunks may be packed."

Wikke held her arm.

"What a hot-headed little rogue," he said, jestingly, his voice husky from the wine. "Wait, sweetheart, and try whether I'll tell. I assure you that you never heard anything quite so base. Yes, Brand is a rascally fellow, but we must laugh at it, for no head so clever will deck the gallows. And he's nearly ready for them. Ha, ha, ha!"

"And the story?" said Heloise, forcing herself to endure his presence.

"Yes, the story," stammered Wikke, raising the glass again to his lips. "The story was a good one. Baroness von Rotterswyl, the black ghost with the pretty daughter, was young once herself, and said to have been as beautiful as the girl who is worshiped by the handsome Prince of the Mill. You probably know about that, eh? Yes, yes! She was visiting a friend in some owl's nest of a castle. I've forgotten the name. And this friend was betrothed to our Doctor Brand; but he wasn't known by that name then—no, indeed; he called himself 'Herr Count.' Moreover, he had lived in Stuttgart as though he had the wealth of the Indies at his disposal. Where he got his ducats Beelzebub could tell better than I. Old Baroness von Rotterswyl loved the brother of this fortunate *fiancée*, a young dandy, named Lewin, if my memory serves me. But one day the bomb burst. Brand took a fancy to the beautiful diamonds of his future—"

"Aha!" said Heloise.

"And absconded with the jewels and ready money. The aforesaid Lewin met him in the forest and stopped him. The fellow had keen eyes, and recognized the masked count; but the latter, too, was no fool, thought 'dead men tell no tales,' drew a pistol, shot his beloved brother-in-law and made tracks as fast as possible. Ah! But Frau von Rotterswyl is said to have spit fire and flame and given the alarm to the authorities, who fairly tumbled over one another. But it was no use; all the clever gentry were forced to give up the chase; the count fooled them. That was nearly twenty years ago. Brand is tolerably well along in life, but he paints and dyes in order to pass for thirty. The whole affair has been forgotten long ago, and is probably outlawed. The fellow even had the insolence to call upon Madam von Rotterswyl. But it seems to me that she must have smelled a rat. At any rate, Brand feels a strong inclination to become a citizen of America. There, that's the whole story!" Wikke drew a long breath and gazed around him with dazed eyes. He had spoken in a loud, excited tone. Now his heavy tongue almost refused to obey his will. "I can't help laughing when I think of the rascally trick. An utterly worthless fellow; but he has brains—brains which can't be matched, and —you see, sweetheart— Where is my glass? Fill it, little one, to the very brim."

He groped over the table with an unsteady hand, and his trembling fingers poured the last drops from the bottle. A broad red stream stained the white table-cloth, and he dropped heavily back into his chair. His red head, with its glazed eyes, sank on his breast, his hoarse laugh became an unintelligible gurgle, and soon deep, rattling breathing announced that friend Wikke had gone to dreamland.

Heloise gazed at the sleeper a moment with loathing. Then hastily approaching him, her trembling hands searched his breast-pocket. Yes—a letter-case. Heloise seized it with sparkling eyes, and examined the contents. A low cry of delight, and she began to scrutinize notes, letters and memoranda. This lasted long enough to give the sleeper the rest he needed. Then she rose, locked the precious pocketbook and its contents in her writing-desk, went up to the drunken man and shook him.

"Herr Wikke!" she shrieked into his ear. "Herr Wikke!"

He started and gazed around him with a stupid stare, then passed his hand across his brow and pondered.

"Surely I haven't been asleep, mademoiselle?" he stammered in an embarrassed tone.

"You have been nodding a little," she said, smiling pleasantly. "It was excusable in the sultry atmosphere and with the strong wine. I was to blame for not giving you a lighter drink."

"Oh, I shall never forgive myself," he said confusedly, trying to stagger to his feet. She waved her hand to check him, and brought a glass of water from a side-table.

"Take a sip; you will feel better."

He hastily emptied the glass.

"Oh, how my head aches!" he groaned.

"Would you like to cool your face a little?" she asked, sympathizingly. "I'll get some fresh water." She went to the next room and filled a basin, then brought it in with a towel. "Don't trouble yourself, Herr Wikke," she said, gayly. "One good friend must help another."

The gray-haired man poured forth a flood of thanks, and Heloise went into the next room to listen, with an ironical smile, as the "good friend" dipped his red head into the refreshing water.

Just at that moment the clock struck half-past seven.

"By King Artus, half-past seven already!" cried Wikke. "I must go to Brand at once. I beg a thousand pardons, mademoiselle. I am frantic over this accident, and cannot imagine how I could forget myself so far. My stupidity—"

"Don't trouble yourself any further about the matter," said his hostess, indulgently. "But if I may advise you, say nothing about it to Brand; he might tease you most unmercifully. Don't tell him you were here; it would be more agreeable to me. Are you better?"

"Perfectly myself again," he answered with a low bow. "But the recollection of my want of tact will be a source of lasting pain."

"Nonsense!" she answered, laughing. "You see that I haven't taken offense. But go, if you have an engagement, and come soon to report your recovery."

Wikke took his departure, and Heloise laughed gayly.

"Oh, thrice-praised Tokay! Yonder fool hasn't the least idea what a secret he has betrayed!"

CHAPTER XVII.

ONE STEP NEARER.

Baroness von Rotterswyl had remained in Wiesbaden alone, sending Marie to visit a friend in Stuttgart, in response to Countess Raven's earnest desire to make the young girl's acquaintance. She had not hesitated to give her consent, for the change wrought in Marie by Gerrald's departure had not escaped her keen eyes. Change of scene, new relations and faces must efface the impression produced by the handsome Prince of the Mill and the parting.

It was a bright, sunny morning. Frau von Rotterswyl sat at the window, reading. Suddenly a low knock at the door interrupted her.

"A lady wishes to see you on urgent business," said the maid.

The baroness looked up in surprise.

"Admit her," she said, curtly, fixing her gray eyes somewhat curiously upon the door.

A dainty figure appeared, richly and tastefully dressed, with waves of raven-black hair clustering around her forehead, and the prettiest little feet which had ever approached the aristocratic lady.

"Pardon my intrusion, baroness," said the stranger, in a pleasantly modulated voice. "It will seem bold, perhaps somewhat indiscreet for me to trouble you, yet I believe I am acting in your interest by making you acquainted with certain matters, madam!"

The baroness's eyes measured the visitor keenly. The piquant little face attracted her, but it was unfamiliar, and she could not recollect having seen the elegant costume, whose sea-green hue could not fail to impress the memory.

"If you have called upon me in regard to a personal matter, madam," she replied with a formal bow, "I can only express my gratitude for the interest you feel in a stranger. At least I cannot recall having made your acquaintance, and, if I have done so, I must beg you to assist my imperfect memory."

"I am Heloise Chênois," said the dancer, with a slight bend of the head, "and certainly have never had the honor of meeting Baroness von Rotterswyl."

"And what do you desire?" asked the baroness,

haughtily. A name from the play-bills fairly froze her blood.

"May I ask you to hear me patiently, madam?" said Heloise, advancing a few steps nearer. "I repeat, that the matter I have to discuss is a serious and important one."

The baroness silently pointed to a chair. All sorts of fancies darted through her brain. What could this person want of her? She could not understand.

"Permit me first to ask a few questions," the Frenchwoman began, leaning lightly on the carved back of the seat. "Did you know in your youth Madam von B——, the widow of an officer who lived for some years in Stuttgart?"

"Certainly," replied the baroness in astonishment. "But where, if I may ask—"

"Let me go on," interrupted the dancer, with a modest but very resolute gesture. "I will relate the following incidents merely to show that I am aware of them, that you may credit the remainder of what I have to say. This lady was betrothed to a Count Berndt, who accompanied her on a visit to her brother Lewin at Castle H——."

"Yes," nodded the old lady.

"And this brother—pardon my indiscretion, baroness—was secretly betrothed to you."

Baroness von Rotterswyl shrank back, her face

blanched to the hue of her cambric handkerchief. An almost terrified look rested upon the dancer.

"That is also true," she said in a hollow tone.

"Count Berndt was a swindler," Heloise curtly added. "He stole his *fiancée's* jewels and money, and shot his brother-in-law in the forest."

"Girl!" shrieked the old baroness, "where did you learn dramas which occurred before your birth, of which no whisper ever reached the world—"

"Have patience!" said Heloise, gently loosing the hand which the baroness had clenched upon her arm. "True, no one knew who had murdered the unfortunate Lewin. The poachers had shot him— was not that the rumor? But I know. No trace of the traitor was found; he was searched for in vain. Ida died of grief because she could not survive the condemnation of the man she loved."

Baroness von Rotterswyl pressed her handkerchief to her eyes. Everything grew dark before them.

"It will soon be twenty years," the dancer continued, "and the story has been forgotten, like the two victims resting in their graves. My home is in Burgundy, and in my country it is said that a murdered man can find no rest until the deed has been expiated. Tell me, baroness, are you at peace, without having found the criminal and without knowing that he is punished? Does your heart feel no longing for revenge, or has it passed away?"

"Passed away!" cried the baroness, almost bitterly. "So long as this heart still beats it will have no other thought."

"And do you hope to fulfill your vow? You have some suspicion, have you not?"

Heloise gazed keenly into the old lady's eyes; her voice sounded hollow and menacing.

The baroness started up from her chair. A terrible thought flashed through her brain. This woman knew Brand; she was his sweetheart—his spy—sent to examine her. Her reply was a haughty rebuff.

"Suspicion, mademoiselle? Why should I? True, I have one that you have come here from other motives than mere interest in me. Do not imagine that the years have dimmed my eyes. They are still keen enough, thank Heaven, to see through the plans of my fellow-mortals."

She turned her back upon her with almost insulting contempt.

"And yet you are mistaken, baroness," replied Mademoiselle Chênois, with a quiet smile. "I assure you that I stand before you as a friend. So you have no suspicion? Very well; I have! Ay, I even *know* who stole the jewels; I know Count Berndt's real name; I know who shot the baron in the forest, and I know the hand that wore Ida's betrothal ring!"

The old noblewoman confronted her like a pallid ghost, with dilated eyes and hands clenched so convulsively that they pressed the delicate cambric handkerchief into a mere wisp.

"You know all this?" she shrieked, with savage exultation. "You know—you know him?"

"Yes," said Heloise, gravely; "and I know, too, that long ago you cherished some suspicion; that you closely watched the false count—I mean Brand!"

"Brand!" repeated the baroness, in a terrible voice. "Brand! Where did you learn all these things, child? Where are your proofs—your witnesses?"

"I can produce no witness, or at best only a confederate and fellow-knave!" said the dancer, with flashing eyes. "But I have one proof in my hands. Convince yourself, baroness, whether those lines could have been written by any other person than the ex-Count Berndt!"

She drew from her pocket a scrap of paper and unfolded the rustling letter.

Baroness von Rotterswyl snatched it from her hand with passionate haste and read, in agitated tones:

"Old pal, I shall be with you in Wiesbaden to-morrow, and bring the whole party, Gerrald, the aristocratic little goose, also old Lady Rotterswyl. Her presence isn't particularly agreeable.

I would rather have the secret spy a hundred miles off, or, better still, with her former lover in the ancestral tomb! Her memory appears to be better than I expected."

The sheet shook in the baroness's fingers; she gazed fixedly at it, then let it fall.

"I thank you, Mademoiselle Chênois," she said, holding out her hand to the dancer. "I beg your pardon for offending you just now."

It was the first time in Baroness von Rotterswyl's life that she had ever asked forgiveness—and now she appealed for it to a ballet-dancer!

"But I hope you will solve this mystery entirely. I understand the enigma only in part," she continued. "Where did you get this letter?"

"It fell into my hands by accident," said Heloise, calmly. "An intimate friend of the writer, to whom the letter was addressed, dropped it out of his case. I found it under his chair after he had gone."

"And how did you learn the whole connection of the affair?" continued the baroness.

"From the same source. Herr Wikke had drunk some of my Tokay and, in consequence, became communicative."

"I have heard that Brand was your friend and confidant, mademoiselle?"

There was still a tone of suspicion in the old lady's voice.

"He was also your friend Ida's confidant," said Heloise, shrugging her shoulders. "He knew that I had jewels, and came for love of my diamonds."

"He has robbed you?"

"Yes, madam!"

"You have reported it?"

The dancer smiled bitterly.

"He is too clever a swindler to commit common theft. No, he compelled me to give him a written statement that I had bestowed the jewels upon him as payment for a trivial friendly service. It was a mere pretext, for I am sure that, had he given me even a glass of water, I should have been forced to sign the paper. He put his hand on his breast-pocket, saying: 'Do either this or that;' and I knew that he would be capable of anything, and that the pistol he carried was loaded! I was obliged to submit, if I wished to escape being murdered! Revenge induced me to lure from his friend the secret concerning you, madam."

The Frenchwoman spoke as lightly as though the whole matter was a trifle, unpleasant, it is true, but not to be changed. Baroness von Rotterswyl had heard of the magnificent jewels, and was astonished at this cool reception of the loss.

"Shameful!" she exclaimed, pacing hurriedly up and down the room. "But how is he to be captured, mademoiselle? The man is as smooth and slippery as an eel, and I fear we can hardly trust solely to the letter, though it is certainly the same handwriting. Let us see, I have some of Ida's old letters."

She went to the chest of drawers, opened the one in the middle, took out an old-fashioned portfolio and hurriedly ransacked its contents, which consisted principally of letters, yellowed sheets, arranged with a certain degree of care.

"Here, look yourself," she exclaimed, exultingly taking out a letter to compare it with Brand's. "Precisely the same hand, only here a little more hurried and careless."

The dancer hastily approached.

"Adored Ida," "Old Pal." Yes, there was a striking resemblance in the handwriting.

"I have other things to reveal, madam," she said in a more excited tone than before, "which would surely place Brand in the hands of the police. It is a secret which may cost him his life. He is a sharper; he is the head of a secret gaming-hell; he treads forbidden paths, and the police seem to be already on his track. He is—"

"Mademoiselle!" cried the baroness, with vehement emotion, pausing before the visitor. "Is this the truth?"

Heloise laid her hand upon her heart.

"I swear it, for I have read it in his own hand."

As she spoke, she gave the baroness another letter from Brand to Wikke.

The baroness read it eagerly and quickly. Then, with a long breath, she straitened herself, pressing her clenched hand upon her breast.

"Now, we have won the game!" she murmured, her eyes blazing with hate. "Oh, my God, how I thank Thee for this hour!"

"The main thing in the whole matter is haste, madam," said Heloise, urgently. "If we wish to accomplish anything, we must act promptly and seize the nest before the birds have fled. Brand, as you see from the letter, will play only two evenings more, and then secretly make his escape to America, so it would be advisable for us instantly to take steps to prevent his eluding us."

"You are right," said Baroness von Rotterswyl, rising. "Come, then, I will dress and hope that you will drive with me to the office of the chief of police."

"I will accompany you, madam!"

While waiting for the baroness, Heloise gazed triumphantly at the green foliage before the window.

"Only have patience, my diamonds. I will soon come for you."

CHAPTER XVIII.

REVENGE.

"This will be the last evening," Brand nodded, with an air of satisfaction, as he walked with Wikke toward the gaming-hall. "Then we will go by the night train direct to the North Sea, and I hope to-morrow we shall see the sun rise over Bremen. Deuce take it! I have the travelling fever, and can scarcely wait for the hour of departure to come."

"Dame Fortune shall have six psalms sung to her when we once breathe the sea air," replied Wikke, drawing a long breath. "Satan knows I had a wretched dream last night. Fie! I actually felt the rope cut into my neck, and when I woke, the first thing I did was to touch my throat to try whether the disagreeable knot was still there. It's a very uncomfortable feeling to have the ground sway under your feet."

"Nightmare, my poor fellow," said Brand, forcing a smile, as he involuntarily loosened his cravat with his thumb. " Hanging has gone out of fashion in the nineteenth century, and nobody thinks of cutting throats on account of a little cheating at the card-table."

"Yes, but suppose that story should leak out," interrupted Wikke, glancing timidly around. "You are surrounded by spies here—Baroness von Rotterswyl, for instance."

"Folly!" said Brand, with a gay laugh. "I haven't an atom of fear of the old woman. If she has failed to discover my identity in nearly three months, she won't feel any suspicion during these last six hours. Besides, I have served up various items of news to her recently. Just now she is pursuing a clue in Breslau, like a vulture circling above its prey. The poor province of Silesia is closely watched. No, my boy, Baroness von Rotterswyl will not play the part of Nemesis in this life, and, spite of our mutual antipathy, I'll drain a glass of champagne to her future prosperity. I've already ordered some bottles of wine, and we'll have one more jolly time this evening."

"Have you packed already?"

"Everything except a few trifles to be flung on the top; then I'll close the trunk and say farewell for this time." Brand took his arm and entered the yard of the secret gaming-house. " Baltimore is said to be a very gay place."

He laughed, turned the handle of the door, and passed into the dimly-lighted corridor up to the gambling-rooms.

Visitors gradually arrived. Brand had just arranged the table in the side-room and closed the blinds; the landlord, Kühn, was noiselessly clearing away the remains of the food which had been served.

Most of the guests were mere youths, scarcely beyond boyhood, and were either preparing for the military service or visiting the springs for pleasure. Some, it is true, came from the neighboring universities to spend Saturday and Sunday at Wiesbaden. The majority were children of wealthy people who had credit and property, but, still inexperienced and thoughtless, were easily tempted, and who scarcely understood the meaning of the notes or post-obits which they so willingly gave.

Ere long the gambling was in full swing, and Brand's keen eye watched the cash that he might be sure to have three times as much come in as he paid out. Luck appeared to be decidedly on the side of the bank to-day. Doctor Brand's well-kept hand constantly gathered in piles of glittering coins, and rarely pushed scanty gains across the green table.

A death-like silence pervaded the room, interrupted only by the monotonous tones of the croupier's voice, or the clink of a gold piece falling on the moldering boards.

Suddenly there was a loud noise on the stairs. Heavy footsteps came nearer and nearer. It was impossible that so many guests could have arrived at once.

Brand listened; his pale face bore unmistakable evidences of excitement.

Suddenly he started up, and gazed with shaking limbs at the door opposite, which had just opened. A dark figure, in a cloak and helmet, appeared on the threshold, grasping a drawn sword.

"In the name of the law," said a deep voice, "you are my prisoners!"

Other police officers followed and hastily surrounded the terrified gamblers, who stared, with blanched faces, at these unbidden guests. Then the momentary paralysis ceased, and was followed by great confusion, amid which all rushed to the windows. In vain. The room was in the second story. The young men, fairly crazed by desperation, dashed forward to force their way through the ranks of the officers. Brand and Wikke darted to the side-door. The former tore it open with trembling hands; a drawn sword flashed before his eyes and a strong hand clutched his arm. Brand wrenched himself free with almost superhuman effort and rushed back into the room; drops of cold perspiration stood on his brow, and his eyes blazed with the light of insanity in their deep sockets. Taking refuge behind a table, he drew a pistol from his breast-pocket.

"Scoundrel! Wretch!" he muttered, through his set teeth, as the men pressed toward him. "I'll shoot down like a dog the first person who dares to touch me! The devil knows I've no idea of jesting. Kühn! Wikke!" he roared, clenching his fist. "Where is Kühn?"

The officers fell back a moment before the madman who was brandishing the pistol at them. The trigger snapped under his fingers, and his eyes rolled with savage resolution. Wikke had already been arrested and led out of the room. Brand leaned against the wall, his face blanched to the hue of death, his white teeth glittered between his drawn lips. The policemen had formed a circle round the croupier, while a lieutenant turned to the trembling gamblers, who, with quiet resignation, awaited their fate.

A compassionate expression hovered around the officer's lips as he noted the reputable names of the boyish prisoners. Then he was obliged to direct his whole attention to Doctor Brand, who, with savage threats, maintained his place. A painful pause followed. The men hesitated to advance toward the murderous bullet. Just at that moment the door of the room opened, and a woman's figure crossed the threshold. She was muffled in gloomy black draperies, which trailed over the floor; her thin face looked like colorless marble amid the folds of a black lace scarf, and a pair of staring gray eyes rested upon the prisoner, who suddenly staggered back, lowering his weapon. The baroness slowly advanced; her noiseless approach seemed to the horrified man like that of a specter. With a gesture of terrible accusation, she raised her slender hand and, in a hollow tone, addressed the man, who, with tangled hair, leaned trembling and powerless against the whitewashed wall.

"Max Zaubinger, Count Berndt and Doctor Brand, in the presence of these witnesses, I make my charge against you. I accuse you of murder, for with this bullet"—the baroness held the bit of lead high aloft—"you killed the brother of your betrothed bride, Baron Lewin! With the same hand you robbed his sister of her jewels and property, forged a will and a certificate of death in Holland, and, in Eastern Prussia, the birth-year of the dead Max Brand in the church register."

"Lies, infamous lies!" shrieked Brand, foaming with rage. "The woman is mad, raving crazy!" By a last effort of resolve, he raised the pistol.

"Make way—or, so help me Satan, a corpse will lie here."

"Calm yourself, doctor!" replied the baroness, in a tone of icy contempt. "If you think a double murder will secure a better fate, you are mistaken. Eleven men will be left to arrest you, if one of their number falls a victim. So cease these vain threats, which will be of no avail. Am I raving? Look, sir. Do you know this letter, do you know who accuses and denounces himself?"

Brand's eyes stared at the page his gloomy accuser held out to him. Black shadows danced before his eyes, and his heart fairly stopped beating. How came this damning sheet into the hands of his enemy? With a gurgling laugh he staggered back against the wall; now he perceived that all hope was indeed over. Then a terrible thought flashed through his brain. With sudden resolution he aimed his weapon at the head of the baroness, but the sergeant's sword-blade darted still more swiftly through the air, and, with a sudden blow, struck down the menacing barrel. There was a loud report, a cloud of smoke, and Brand fell forward heavily against the sharp edge of the table.

The smoke floated around the tops of the helmets. The oil-lamps flickered dimly above the head of the baroness, who, her figure drawn to its full height, still stood with uplifted hand. Not a muscle in the stony face quivered. Why should she tremble before the hand which had robbed her of every joy in life?

Close by the wall lay a dying man, still gasping faintly, his limbs twitching in the last agony. The black-robed figure slowly advanced and gazed intently at the hated features, from which the rude hand of death had stripped the mask. The profile of "Count Berndt" was relieved with horrible distinctness against the floor, waxen, pale and scarcely disfigured, but without its perpetual smile. The hand still clenched the pistol, and from the temple a dark stream trickled down the whole shirt, crimsoning the breast just at the spot where the fatal bullet had struck the hapless Lewin.

"The murderer has executed himself, baroness," said the captain of police. "Your accusation was swiftly followed by justice."

The lady stood motionless before the lifeless form, then, with silent horror, she stepped back, clasping her slender hands:

"Thy ways are long and wonderful, oh, God, but they lead to the goal—to vengeance and retribution!"

She bowed her head in prayer, then turned and, with a formal greeting, passed noiselessly through the door.

Meanwhile Heloise had watched the course of

events from the next room. She saw that Brand was shot, and glided swiftly into the little corridor. His overcoat must hang there. She groped her way to it and hastily searched the pockets, where she found a large door-key and a bunch of small keys. Grasping her prize with delight, she hurried swiftly down the stairs into the darkness.

Without a single backward glance, Heloise rushed through the deserted streets to Brand's lodgings and, opening the door, ran up the carpeted stairs to his room. She tried the key; her fingers trembled, but she clenched her teeth, opened the creaking lock and, almost blind with excitement, stepped into the room.

The trunk stood in the center, unlocked—so much the better! Heloise raised the lid and rummaged with feverish haste among the various articles it contained, tossing them hither and thither. Then she uttered a low cry of delight. Her casket! Her casket!

Snatching the treasure, she pressed it to her panting breast and fled swiftly from the dead man's abode.

Darting under the rustling trees in the park, she glided through the shadows and reached home, breathless. There she set the casket down and lighted the gas—all the jets which she could find; she wanted to have the room as bright as though the sun was shining into it with full radiance.

"Triumph!" she exclaimed, with rapturous delight, loosening her wealth of dark hair. She was standing before the mirror, longing to enjoy the sight of her resplendent image! What a glow of light the chandelier poured down upon her! Now for her jewels—her diamonds!

She went to the casket, pressing her hand upon her beating heart, her eyes closed a moment, as if she was afraid of being blinded by the flash of the diamonds—the spectacle of the idolized treasure to which her whole soul clung! Then she slowly raised the lid. A startled cry followed, and Heloise, staggering back, sank fainting beside the crimson-lined jewel case. It was—empty!

CHAPTER XIX.

IN THE ENEMY'S COUNTRY.

The mist hung like a damp pall over the neighboring forest; the broad plain lay veiled and formless, separated from a patch of land recently cleared by a long row of fir-trees. The moon was pale, no star shone brightly through the gray clouds, which hung in a mass as heavy and threatening as though all the smoke of the cannon used in the war had risen heavenward to utter complaints and lamentations.

The wind swept by, tossing the swaying branches, whose gay autumnal foliage whirled down to the damp earth; the plaintive notes of birds echoed from the neighboring rushes, and died away in a soft echo in the western valley. Wooded mountain-peaks stood forth in sharp relief against the sky; the mysterious notes of the alarm-bell accompanied the red light on the clouds with appeals for help; yonder flamed the cruel torch swung by the fleshless hand of war.

Here, too, in the little woodland meadow flames were blazing, but the light they shed was peaceful, and the scene which they illumined was full of repose—the bivouac of the hussars. The guards paced to and fro; their steps died away on the moss-covered ground, and nothing was heard save the clank of the sabers when their wearers passed over projecting roots, or the loose stones grated under their tread.

The men, worn out by the long ride, lay sleeping heavily on wretched beds made of scanty bundles of rain-soaked straw, with their cloaks wrapped about them. They were sturdy Germans, among them many members of the Landwehr, called to arms from the most varied trades, and lulled to sweet dreams of their native land by the spicy odor of the surrounding forest.

The officers were gathered around one of the fires. A flask was passed from hand to hand, and in the midst of the circle was spread a chart of the country, which was eagerly discussed and studied, and frequently crossed with colored pencil-marks.

The adjutant was silently tracing upon the chart an almost imperceptible path through the mountains.

"Poor fellow!" he murmured under his breath.

"The path can scarcely be found upon the chart, and to follow it on a dark night in an entirely unknown country! It's two o'clock, major," he cried, looking up. "They must have reached headquarters by this time, if the way was open."

The major drew out his watch.

"Yes, they may be there. Indeed, they may have reached their destination long ago," he added, gravely; "but who can tell where our brave fellows may be fighting! The ride was at the risk of life, and I almost fear that Gerrald pays too little heed to the danger which surrounds him—knows no caution in his zeal. Have you found any by-paths, Haldern?"

"Two cross-roads, major."

A pause ensued. The gentlemen were grave and absorbed in their own thoughts as, sitting silently side by side, they puffed clouds of smoke from their short pipes.

The wind roared through the neighboring forest, tossing the boughs to and fro. A wan moonbeam stole through the clouds, and the alarm-bell, with a last shrill note, ceased to sound. It was an uncanny night.

"It would be a sad pity for Gerrald," murmured Lieutenant von Haldern between his set teeth. "So brave a soldier deserves to die on the field of honor, and not be treacherously shot from ambush, like hunted game. These beastly *Franc-tireurs* infest the whole region, and, by heaven, it's no child's play to slip through their line."

"Even if our brave comrade should not return," interposed one of the captains, "he will probably die the most honorable death of any of us. In the open field the soldier has his enemy before him; he knows where Death grins at him and does not fear his dart; but Gerrald volunteered for a ride during which every step may be his last, where danger threatens on all sides, and before which our boldest men quailed. It was necessary to carry to headquarters the news that the enemy was advancing in strong force, unnoticed; if he obtained free passage all was lost. Thanks to the bold spy and our friend Gerrald's excellent glass, we perceived the maneuver in time, and, I hope, shall now be able to thwart the clever plan."

Meantime the smothered beat of horses' hoofs was heard amid the neighboring thicket; the branches snapped and rustled; now and then a saber clanked. Impatient snorting and the noise of pebbles dashed aside reached the ears of the officers; then the dewy moss subdued the sound, and nothing was heard except the pattering of the rain-drops shaken from the drooping boughs.

The sentinel challenged.

"Lieutenant Gerrald and ten hussars returned

from orderly duty," replied the young officer's familiar voice.

The troop of cavalry turned into the meadow, and their leader sprang from his steaming horse and hastily advanced toward the group of officers, who had started up and rushed to meet him.

"Where in the world did you come from?" asked several voices in astonishment. But the young man stood erect before his superior officer, raised his hand to his cap in a military salute, and briefly gave his report.

The flickering fire cast a vivid light upon his handsome features and flashed upon his saber swinging at his side.

"I thank you, Lieutenant Gerrald," replied the major, with a tremor of feeling in his gruff tones. "I thank you in the name of our country. You have saved the lives of many brave comrades, and aided our illustrious sovereign, if it is God's will, to a fresh victory! So the order to advance is given, the battle will come at last, and I believe, gentlemen, that we are on the eve of an important day. Your hand, Gerrald. What? Are you wounded?"

Haldern hastened forward and raised the limp arm, in whose place Gerrald had offered his left hand, while the other members of the group pressed around him with eager questions.

"Were you forced to cut your way through the enemy? Have you had a skirmish?"

The young officer made an involuntary effort to raise the wounded limb.

"We met the men in blouses!" he muttered between his set teeth, with flashing eyes. "We were obliged to leave two fine fellows yonder in the mountains. Corporal Höcker has received a severe wound in the head, and three horses are injured; but the darkness prevented my determining to what extent. Sergeant Meissner's little bay limps badly. I received a slash in the arm as a memento; it's a mere trifle, but it makes it useless."

He turned and held out his sound hand to Haldern and his other comrades.

"How are you, gentlemen! I almost thought, up yonder in the woods, that we should never say good evening to one another again!"

His voice sounded blithe and cordial.

"So there was a sharp skirmish?" cried a young officer, springing across a bundle of straw to offer his field flask. "By Jove, Gerrald, you are a lucky fellow! I am quite sure any one of us would have bit the dust, and you alone, as Fortune's favorite child, escaped with barely a scratch. There he stands now as quietly as though nothing of the least importance had happened, and yet he as good as has the iron cross in his pocket. The major doesn't say much usually, but to-day—" He glanced with a significant gesture at his superior officer, who, accompanied by the surgeon, had gone to the returned hussars to examine their various wounds.

"So the bomb will burst to-morrow!" a first lieutenant called across the fire. "Well, any battle in the open field will be more welcome than this confounded work in the woods, where the utmost that can be expected is to get a murderous bit of lead in the ribs. So you encountered the band in the woods and sharpened your swords on one another's bones in the true barbarous fashion of ancient times. How strong were they?"

"Probably twice our number," replied Gerrald, shrugging his shoulders.

Haldern gravely interrupted.

"I had confidently expected that you would remain at headquarters until to-morrow. To make such an expedition twice in one night augurs more than contempt of death, and I am also perfectly sure that you returned to us by your own wish."

Gerrald gazed gloomily into vacancy.

"The order to march had to be brought to-night, for we are to join the infantry in E—— at eight o'clock to-morrow morning, and, consequently, we must leave here at five at the latest. The general wished to send a party of dragoons; but what was the use of having the poor fellows wander about in this wilderness, where they would never have found their way down into the valley! I had already gone through the difficulties, and knew the ground, while they were ignorant of it. No, that would have been useless waste of life! My men ride like the Wild Huntsman; the horses were still fresh; so why should others dash into needless destruction? Therefore I volunteered to return."

"I hope the general understood the meaning of the offer?" said Von Haldern, with sparkling eyes. "I presume he was satisfied with his hussars?"

"He thanked me in the name of the king and assured me of his fullest appreciation," replied Gerrald, quietly nodding assent. "But I really don't understand why you make such an ado over my doing my duty. I consider it a matter of course."

"Go and cool your arm now; the hand is very much swollen," said the captain of the regiment, who had returned with the major. "You will probably be unable to use anything but a revolver tomorrow, Gerrald; it's a bad cut."

"And I advise you to get a few hours' sleep, my brave young fellow," added the commander, holding out his hand to him a second time. "Corporal Höcker and Meissner have given me the details of your skirmish, and I can only express my entire satisfaction with your discreet management. I congratulate you, comrade, and shall propose your name as a loyal soldier for the bestowal of the iron cross."

Gerrald silently bowed his thanks. A deep flush crimsoned his brow, and his mournful eyes sparkled with the proud delight of the young warrior who gathers his first laurels from the thorny, blood-soaked ground.

Haldern thrust his arm into his friend's and drew him away to the camp-fire. His brother officers pressed with sincere pleasure around their universally popular comrade, and they finally exchanged a "good-night"—perhaps the last. There was something in the clasp of the hand which suggested an eternal farewell. There is a strange feeling concerning the parting on the eve of a battle. Who knows whether to-morrow evening one can clasp a hand warm with life?

So they parted and laid their weary heads to rest beside the crackling fire. It sounded as familiar as at their beloved homes, and pitying dreams conjured around their damp couches the dear forms far away in their distant native land.

Haldern and Gerrald still sat together. The fire had almost burned out; only a bright flash occasionally blazed upward, flickering over the faces of the two men who were conversing so earnestly together.

Leo von Haldern had a peculiar temperament.

whose almost gloomy bias made him appear several years older. A series of misfortunes and the loss of the woman whom he loved had embittered his youth and prematurely ripened him to manhood, frequently rendering life a necessity hard to endure. His features were pale, finely-chiseled, and marked with the lines of fate. He was a quiet, thoughtful man, whose frequent melancholy formed a strange contrast to his companions' gay spirits, and which doubly attracted him to Gerrald, whose reserve touched a sympathetic chord. Their friendship was a slow growth, but it was a bond formed for life, which made the young men as intimate as brothers. Haldern was a man of brilliant intellect, whose talents and knowledge were gladly recognized and appreciated. He served his country better with his brains than with his blade, whose keenness he had not yet had an opportunity to test. Compared with his excitable friend, he possessed a calm, reflective character, quietly repaired many an error which the hot-headed Gerrald committed, and yet bestowed upon the young officer, though so much his junior, his warmest admiration and friendship. His passionate longing for conflict and peril impressed him ; the daring boldness with which he made his reconnoitering expeditions affected him as much as it won the admiration of his comrades ; and the success which frequently attended his efforts, and gained for him the esteem and regard of his superior officers, rendered Haldern as proud and happy as though he himself was the bold rider. Gerrald was an original sort of fellow, and his fearlessness frequently bordered upon a strange defiance of danger, when he essayed to push a perilous situation to extremes.

Yet Haldern's keen eye did not fail to perceive that this scorn of death and exposure of his own life was from a morbid desire to court the perils of war as much as possible, that he was constantly throwing down the gauntlet to death, and yet had constantly escaped, frequently in a very remarkable way. The young baron even understood his friend's dreams and thoughts when, at the close of a day of wild excitement, he was left to himself and his reveries; and after gazing mournfully into the distance, he buried his face in his hands with a gesture of despair, after covering the sealed mystery which he wore day and night like a talisman upon his heart with fervent kisses.

"Gerrald," the adjutant began, fixing his dark eyes earnestly upon his friend's features, "this is, perhaps, the last time I shall see you. What may have befallen us by to-morrow evening, we do not know, and I have a sad foreboding that I must tell you everything which burdens my heart to-day, since I may not be able to do so to-morrow."

Gerrald pressed the speaker's hand, and gazed silently into the ruddy glow at his feet.

"You have been my best and truest friend, Traugott," Von Haldern added, in an agitated tone. "I have loved few persons, and been loved by few. I have never known happiness. Death robbed me of all that I held dear; you are the only soul who has understood me; you have often shared my grief and been silent concerning your own life. I have never asked the cause of your mysterious conduct, have never tortured you with questions, as a friend may be permitted to do, because I was afraid of being indiscreet. This is, perhaps, the last time that we shall have the sky above our heads. Take no secret into the grave, Gerrald. Reveal it."

The young officer raised his eyes sorrowfully.

"I have no secret, Leo," he said, in a hollow tone. "On the contrary, too many already know it; that is why I keep silence. What you desire to learn is quickly told; the words containing so much misery are absurdly few. I made a vow and broke it. I possessed the love of a woman of angelic purity and forfeited it. I deserted a ballet-dancer and she revenged herself upon me, and now I wish to offer my life in expiation, and Death disdains it; or has hitherto. What the morrow will bring I do not know."

He supported his head on his hand and gazed

fixedly at his sword, whose point was jagged and stained. Raising the slender steel blade, he tested the point with his thumb.

"It has done me many a good service," he murmured; "hold out bravely to-morrow, old friend."

Haldern made no reply; he seemed lost in thought. The leaves rustled, a horse snorted, and a sentinel's saber clanked against the roots and stones.

Leo raised his head.

"Does she no longer love you?" he asked, in a low tone.

Gerrald drew his treasure from his pocket.

"Look; she gave me this when we parted; a talisman that is to protect me. Then we bade each other farewell. I do not know what it is. I cannot open it until I am severely wounded or can replace it in her hands at the close of the campaign. Does she love me? Yes, she said so, though perhaps it was an act of charity, of mercy, not to let the man who once possessed her heart depart without a blessing. Oh, Haldern!" he groaned, pressing his hand upon his breast in the torture of his suffering. "Why must I drag out this burdensome existence, of which I am utterly weary?"

"Do not sin, Gerrald; you are standing on the verge of the grave every instant!" said Haldern, passing his arm around his friend's neck. "And if you survive to-morrow, show that you are still worthy —to live."

The fresh morning breeze swept over the meadow and drove the mist into the valley; Haldern drew his cloak closer around his shoulders and pushed a bundle of straw under his head.

"Let us rest an hour, comrade," he said. "We shall need fresh strength to-morrow, and it will be so pleasant to be waked once more by the bright sunshine."

"You speak as though you had ordered a bullet specially for your heart," said Gerrald, trying to jest. "No, we will not say good night to each other, friend Leo. God grant that the sun may shine in your eyes for many a year!"

A tender clasp of the hand, then all was still around the fire; its coals yet glimmered under the ashes; the blades of grass waved to and fro, a faint light tinged the sky, and the sentinel on the edge of the forest hummed softly under his breath:

"Then I think of my distant love,
Whether she tender and true will prove."

CHAPTER XX.

A MEETING.

The sun set, blood-red. It had witnessed much misery during that day's course, been reflected in many a dim eye, and drunk from the earth with its burning rays many a soldier's heart's blood; now it was sinking to rest, casting a shimmering farewell light upon the sleepers whose cold hearts will rest on the morrow beneath the cool earth. They slumbered soundly and forever—the brave champions of God and their native land!

The battle was over. Deep peace brooded over the broad field of conflict. A distant signal, a neighing steed, dashing riderless across the plain, were the only sounds, save an occasional death-rattle.

Gerrald slowly raised himself; his bewildered gaze rested on the sunset glow, wandered over the field of carnage, the corpses and heaps of ruins, then slowly returned to the broken sword at his side. Where was he?

He mechanically pressed his hand upon his shoulder. The warm blood trickled over his finger, staining his dusty uniform. Gradually consciousness returned, and, with a deep sigh, he looked at the aching wound. So he was still alive! He lay bleeding upon the deserted field. Where were his comrades? Where was Haldern? Yes, now he remembered how they had fought—dashed against the hostile square. He saw Haldern fall from his horse; pressed forward to lift the dying man; he saw the foe dash down upon him; raised his pistol; beheld the enemy fall; then his own horse sank under him; he worked his way out from beneath the animal's weight; his arm fell powerless; something struck him; then all was darkness. But where was Haldern? Did he still live? Had he escaped?

Traugott felt his strength revive. Turning his head, he gazed searchingly around. There lay the Frenchman whom he had shot, and a few paces off, his horse; but he did not see Haldern. And yet, was not that a hussar uniform among yonder heap of corpses? And there again—and there! Ah! He saw several familiar uniforms.

His heart quivered at the spectacle. He longed to start up, to rush forward, but sank back again, and a terrible pain in his arm and shoulder almost robbed him of consciousness a second time. Groaning heavily, he let his head sink on the ground. The moss cooled his cheeks, and the broken stems of the heather mingled with his tangled hair. Minutes elapsed; then a burning thirst tortured him. He longed for a few drops of some refreshing drink, and feeling for the leather thong which held his field-flask, he raised it with a trembling hand to his lips.

The brandy ran down his throat like fire, seemed to rouse his dormant vitality, and made the blood throb in his temples. Opening the uniform, he tried to strip off the sleeve. Again a stream of blood poured from the wound, dyeing the white ribbon on his breast. The "God guard you" was colored with a crimson stain. Traugott pressed his handkerchief on the wound, and once more attempted to rise, tottering forward a few steps only to fall again. By his side lay the French horseman. The bullet had pierced his breast; a dark stream was also flowing from a wound above his high boots, and his livid lips quivered from the terrible agony he was suffering.

Unutterable sympathy overpowered the young officer. He again loosed his field-flask, bent over the wounded man, and slowly dropped the strengthening liquid on his parched tongue. A long breath heaved the chest, the limbs relaxed as if with a sense of profound relief, and when Traugott unfastened the buttons of the coat and loosened the sword-belt, the cuirassier opened his dim eyes and gazed at the German deliverer who was so mercifully aiding his foe.

An inarticulate murmur reached his ear; the Frenchman's wan hand was feebly raised, and Traugott understood the mute thanks, lifted the wounded man's head to a more comfortable position, and repeatedly moistened his parched tongue. A smile of touching appreciation flitted over his distorted face; then sighing heavily, he closed his eyes, and again lapsed into unconsciousness.

Weakness also overpowered Traugott, who lay gazing blankly at the clouds, whose sunset hues were fading. He arranged his head more comfortably on the moss-covered stone; his hand rested heavily on his breast, closely clasping the mysterious jewel which seemed, in truth, to guard him. Then he looked thoughtfully at the pallid face of the French cavalryman, and the hand which but a few hours ago had wielded the weapon with such youthful vigor now lay clenched upon his bleeding breast.

It was a narrow face, framed by a dark, full beard;

the high forehead was grave and furrowed by lines of thought. Now there was a terrible rigidity in every feature, a marble pallor which yielded only to the deep shadows under the closed eyes—the mysterious banner of Death, which he plants with a rude hand upon the countenances of his victims.

Traugott gazed earnestly at this face, which conjured up a flood of thoughts. Who could he be? Where was his distant home, which would give him no grave beside his loved ones? Whom did he leave behind in unutterable anguish? Perhaps a mother mourning her only child—her comfort, her hope; a mother whose sole joy was in those closed eyes, perhaps never more to open upon the light of this world. Oh, happy son, whose mother can remember him in love and peace, who need never reproach himself with having darkened her life! Or did a betrothed bride await him—a young, loving creature, whom his strong arm was to guide? Will she not weep for him and daily pray for his return? What was her appearance? Did she resemble that one image of maidenhood, fair and thoughtful, gentle and sweet as yonder little wild rose hanging by its broken stem from the bush? Or was she a true child of the Southern sun, laughing and vivacious, mischievous and coquettish amid her wealth of waving brown locks?

Gerrald's head sank lower on his breast. The

figures before his eyes became more indistinct, blending into a misty blur. Only the blossom waving on the rock opposite stood forth distinctly before his eyes, and seemed to be transformed into a girl's rosy face, nodding gently and consolingly to him. The wounded man closed his eyes with a smile, and dreamed of the little wild rose amid the swaying boughs.

Dreary weeks dragged slowly along on leaden wings; weeks alternating between the delusions of fever and death-like exhaustion, and which gave cause for greater apprehension from the sufferer's nervous exhaustion than from the wound itself.

Gerrald was in a hospital. How he had come there he did not know; he only remembered dimly that he had been awakened on the battle-field by the rescuing party, and had stood beside Haldern's corpse to kiss, with deep emotion, the cold brow of his loyal comrade. As he closed his glazed eyes and then sank fainting himself, the nervous fever set in, the surgeon had stated.

Now the worst was over. The struggle between life and death had ended. Gerrald's youth and vigorous constitution had again snatched him from the edge of the grave, beside which he had so often stood without descending into it. Next to his couch was the one occupied by the French cuirassier. It brought a soothing sensation to the young officer to see the familiar features near him. He felt less desolate after recognizing his companion in suffering at his side.

By Traugott's special request the Frenchman had received on the battle-field the prompt and careful aid without which the feeble spark of life would have been long since extinguished; now the young German tended him as one tends a beloved friend whose wishes we seek to read in the eyes ere they are uttered.

The stranger was far too severely wounded to keep pace with Gerrald in his recovery. He could rarely exchange a few words with him—nay, he scarcely recognized his Samaritan of the battle-field; and when consciousness slowly returned, as convalescence progressed, he lay on his couch of pain in gloomy silence, staring mournfully at the clouds of snow which the tempest drove westward. He could never again dance or ride, as if to vie with the little flakes; he had become a cripple; sound and vigorous in mind, but broken in strength in the very prime of life!

It was a gloomy winter evening. The storm raged through the streets, creaking the rusty vane, driving the icy flakes against the panes and heaping them high on the frozen earth, then sweeping them away and spreading them out in a glimmering pall, beneath which all the magnificence and gladness of the wide world lay buried.

An old monastery had been transformed into a hospital, which sheltered in its cells and halls the hapless victims of the dearly-bought victories, which daily brought more sufferers to the House of Mercy.

Traugott lay in a small room on the ground floor, with a Prussian infantry captain. The third companion was the French cuirassier, who became more and more warmly attached to his German neighbor. There was a peculiar charm in approaching with self-sacrificing kindness and friendship the man with whom, a few weeks ago, he had a life-and-death struggle, and studying in his book of life many a noteworthy chapter which reflected the world in hues ever new. What triumph could have been greater than that of making the enemy a friend for life?

Gerrald had learned many incidents of the young Frenchman's past, which contained a portion of the Parisian world, whose changeful scenes formed a piquant romance in the eyes of the grave German. Maurice de Gorcy was the son of aristocratic parents, but having been orphaned at an early age and left in possession of a considerable fortune, he had enjoyed his youth to the full, fluttered through his Parisian Eden, and finally fell in love with a little dancer, far more deeply than he would ever admit. She flirted with him as she did with the rest of her admirers, laughed at him when he attempted to reproach her for her reckless conduct, and pouted scornfully when he talked of marriage. This irritated his proud nature, and he broke with her. She left the country, and Maurice married a member of the aristocracy, the beautiful, idolized *marquise*, who possessed every attraction save a heart to love him. He admired her beauty, without feeling any thrill of affection; endured her caprices without a murmur; shared her triumphs without being jealous. Day by day he became more gloomy, till he was at last called an oddity. Then his wife's conduct suddenly passed beyond the borders of decorum; he roused himself from his indifference, defended the honor of his name, obtained a divorce from his wife, and shot her lover in a duel.

He was now entirely alone in the world; but he did not grieve. He had become too grave to find pleasure in Paris, and so buried himself in the solitude of his estates. There he wandered alone through the woods, without friend or companion. He did not even hunt much; he had no interest in the flying game; but when he saw a glittering lizard glide over the moor, with its bright eyes sparkling through the blades of grass, he thought of his litttle dancer, and sighed deeply at the remembrance.

Then the war came. He hurried back to Paris, and took up arms. While riding through the *boulevards,* chatting with an acquaintance, a branch of laurel fell on the neck of his horse, and a laughing face bent from a carriage an da familiar voice called :

"*Bon jour,* Maurice !"

He again saw his dancer of the *Variétés.* His love surged up again in his heart, stronger, more sincere than ever ; but there was no time to tell her so. And why should he? She probably loved him no better now than in former days. So he went to the war. He wrote to her several times, and constantly expected a few lines in reply ; but in vain. She had probably never received his letters.

"What was the lady's name?" asked Traugott, eagerly.

"Blanche Vertieux," said the cuirassier, dreamily.

"So it was not she," murmured Gerrald. He fancied he must know the dancer, too.

The fire snapped on the hearth ; a little lamp which diffused a flickering light hung from the chimney. The sick-room was silent. Maurice lay asleep ; the captain had stumped out into the hall on his wooden leg to chat with some comrades, or to write letters home, and Traugott lay silently on his cushions, painting sweet visions of the future.

Just at that moment the door noiselessly opened. A woman's slender figure entered, brushing the flakes of snow from her black dress. The hussar did not look up. He thought it was a Sister of Charity, and merely waved his hand toward his sleeping friend.

Then words fell on his ears. A voice asked for Maurice de Gorcy.

The tone of that voice was like an electric shock. He raised himself, stared at the newcomer, and almost shrieked:

"Heloise!"

She, too, tottered back several paces, raising her hands in boundless amazement, then murmured, in a hollow tone:

"You here, Traugott?"

He gazed into her face, which looked pale and narrow, framed in a black veil. The eyes were mournful and surrounded by black circles; the lips were drawn tightly over the white teeth. What had happened to Heloise? She was no longer the same as of yore. No longer the laughing beauty—the Satanella of the D—— stage; but a feeble, fragile woman, standing in her black robes. What could she have experienced to banish from her cheeks the reckless, sunny smile?

"So you are Blanche Vertieux?" cried Gerrald, raising himself. "Oh, I suspected it. I recognized you in every word. No, do not go to him. Maurice has been ill—dangerously ill. He must not see you again so unexpectedly, Blanche Vertieux!"

She slowly approached and gazed mournfully at him.

"Yes, that is my real name, Traugott; though I am known by it only in Paris. So he spoke of me—he expected me?" she went on, excitedly, "Ah, if I have not come this weary way in vain!"

Her eyes met his, which rested gloomily upon her, and he averted his head as she steadily returned the gaze.

"Traugott," she said softly, clasping her hands, "I never expected to meet you again in this life. I did not hope to do so, and now that it has happened I thank God for it."

A heavy sigh escaped her lips, and her eyes rested anxiously on his pallid face. She awaited an answer, but Traugott pressed his lips firmly together and remained silent.

"It has burdened me like some evil spell," Heloise continued, in a trembling voice. "The memory has pursued me like a demon, granting me no peace. I have had no good fortune since I left you, Traugott! Everything has resulted in disaster; everything went wrong, and the star hitherto so favorable set forever in gloomy clouds. The remembrance of our last meeting haunted me as if I had pronounced the curse upon myself, and the hand which hurled your jewel into the lake—"

"Silence!" groaned the wounded man. "Go,

Heloise, go. Why do you cross my path again, if you merely wish to remind me of the hour that poisons my whole existence?"

There was a terrible accusation in the tone of his voice, and Heloise pressed her hand upon her heart with a bitter smile.

"Poisons your whole existence?" she repeated, with an indescribable look. "As if you were the only sufferer, Gerrald—a greater sufferer than the woman who wrecked her own happiness with yours, who is compelled to bear the double torture of the pangs of conscience and of desertion—abandoned alike by God and the world! Do you imagine, Gerrald, that that night left no traces upon me—did not pour into my heart the venom I sought to instill into yours? I have felt every word, every one of those sharp dagger-thrusts with two-fold keenness in my own heart, a heart that cannot forget that it once loved you! I have never wept during my gay life on the stage; never regretted any action; did not even know the bitter taste of tears. Now it seemed as if all the omissions were to be repaired—as if I were now to pass through all these hours of sorrow, hours which had once seemed so absurdly far away. I was to atone doubly for my former mockery. Every form of misery has been heaped upon me during this last year. Oh, God, what experiences I have had! What bitter, bitter want I have endured!"

She covered her face with her hands—thin, transparent white hands.

Traugott raised himself on his pillows; her words pierced him to the heart, and the sight of her stirred him even more powerfully than memory.

"You have suffered want?" he repeated, with dilated eyes. "How can a woman like you suffer want? You, Heloise, who are received everywhere with open arms?"

A sorrowful smile quivered around her lips as she gazed intently at the sleeping cuirassier, who, sighing heavily, turned over on the other side.

"I was ill; robbed; helpless," she continued, in a hollow tone. "No one took my part; I could get no engagement. Matters went from bad to worse. I knew what it was to eat dry bread. Oh! And then the war! This horrible war! I received a letter from Maurice; he was the only human being who still cared for me. I sought him amid all these horrors. I knew that I should find him." She paused again; then, with a swift glance, asked: "Have you, too, been unhappy, Traugott? Unhappy for the sake of a half-withered flower, which the fair-haired baroness could restore at any time? Why is your whole existence poisoned because, in the whirl of the dance, you lost her little pledge of love? Are you still wretched, Traugott? In the name of Heaven's mercy, tell me that it is not so!"

She sank beside his couch; her timid glance pleaded for mercy, and tears streamed upon her clasped hands; the flickering firelight danced over her emaciated features.

"You do not know the association with that flower, Heloise," murmured the young officer, in a hollow tone. "You are mistaken if you think it was a gift from Marie. When I put the flower into the case, I neither knew her nor dreamed how terrible the consequences of such a memento might become."

"Not from Marie?" escaped her lips; her features expressed mortal anxiety. "Good heavens! What was it, then?"

"The last legacy of a dead woman!" said Traugott, with marked emphasis. "The blossom was from my mother's coffin!"

A low cry reached his ears. Heloise was on her knees, with her blanched face hidden in her hands. There was no sound, only a slight tremor shook the black-robed form.

At last she looked up at him, with a strange light sparkling in her eyes.

"Then forgive me, for the sake of my soul, which this flower has saved for the kingdom of heaven!"

Gerrald clasped her hand closely in his own.

"Forgotten and forgiven, Heloise!" he said, gently. "You have faithfully atoned for your error;

and I, too, have passed through darkness into light. Let us part in peace, as friends—friends for time and eternity!"

Heloise had risen, and laid her hand upon his head, as if in benediction.

"Yes, be my friend, Traugott," she pleaded, with a gentle glance. "I am beginning a new life to-day, and God sent me the helping hand which will point out the better path. A butterfly does not stop fluttering to and fro. I am fit neither for a sister nor a nun; but I will be a good, true wife. Yonder sick, crippled man needs aid and sympathy—' She pointed to the wounded officer. "If he does not reject the dancer, she will find in his heart a home where she can accomplish good."

"No—he will not reject her!" exclaimed Traugott, in an agitated tone. "He will welcome the woman who occupies his thoughts night and day, like a weary bird who has flown to and fro long enough!"

"May God grant it," said the little dancer of the *Variétés*. And clasping her hands, she prayed silently. Satanella had laid her golden horns in the grave with her lover.

CHAPTER XXI.

AN EXCELLENT MATCH.

Baroness von Rotterswyl had returned from her visit to Frankfort. She looked somewhat pale and weary, her eyes had a strangely mournful expression, and her gaze was pensive and often dewy with tears. Her mother thought that her daughter's manners were far more finished, and that she had acquired at Countess Raven's entertainments the ease of bearing which a Baroness von Rotterswyl should possess under all circumstances.

Marie uttered a sigh of relief when she again entered her quiet home. This peaceful room, with its bow-window, was so far above the confused tumult of the world, knew naught of all the heartbreak below, and received the young girl like a cozy, hidden nest, whither she could flee with all her sorrows. True, there were no blossoms on the rosebushes in the window; only a few Alpine violets were opening their petals on the sill, and nodded a greeting. The little songsters were still in charge of the bird-seller, and a thick layer of dust rested on the book-shelves; but her old friend in the black frame gazed down at her with the same quiet smile. Ah, did she not suspect how much sorrow her descendant had endured during this time? It cheered Marie to know that she was again near her loyal ancestress. She gazed at the familiar, pallid features of the picture which, through so many long years, had been her sole companion, leaned her head tenderly against the lifeless breast, and for the first time felt thoroughly at home in her secluded nook. Alas, it was a sorrowful meeting—very different from the one Marie had imagined at her departure. Burning tears coursed down her cheeks and wet Barbara Gerrald's portrait.

Little Marie had been away many long months. When she left D——, the fierce sun of July was burning in the heavens, and the whole wide world was full of green foliage and blossoms; every breast was stirred with emotions of happiness, and the heart joined exultantly in the love-song of Nature. And now winter had come. All was cold and desolate, deserted and silent. The wind was tearing the last withered leaves from the trees to the ground, and the snow was falling, covering the bosom of the earth with high white drifts, that the eye might see no trace of former magnificence.

Marie went to the window, melted the glittering

frost-flowers with her breath, and looked across to *his* window, where he had once stood gazing mournfully up at the sky. How long ago that was, and how many changeful scenes life had unrolled between the past and present!

The panes were covered with frost. The ancient house stood before her, rigid and lifeless as a tomb, like the enchanted palace in Uhland's poem, in whose garret chamber white-haired Poesy sits at the buzzing wheel.

Old Gretlis still lived in the lonely building, shadowy and busy as a good spirit weaving thread after thread into the long-desired shroud.

The young baroness gazed thoughtfully across the street, then, with a heavy sigh, rested her head against the window-sash. The sight of the silent house pierced her to the heart, yet she could neither avert her eyes nor turn her thoughts from it. She had heard nothing from young Gerrald for a long time. Whom should she ask? She did not know a single human being in Frankfort whom she could trust; no one was interested in Gerrald, no one knew him. Perhaps Count Hasso might have aided her, but she saw only too soon that it would be useless to apply to him. Besides, she felt a positive aversion to Aunt Raven's idol, and the more the latter praised his talents and, with maternal blindness, lauded the young man to the skies, the more clearly Marie saw the fundamental defects in his character, which were concealed by the superficial varnish of polished manners. She had already seen men of character too wholly unlike to be impressed by this youthful dandy, who too often strove to supply his lack of personal comeliness by the arts of the toilet.

But Count Raven was a good match, and this enabled marriageable beauties to close their eyes, admire him in the most undeserved manner, and constantly inspire the heir of Castle Raveneck with fresh conceit.

His personal appearance was styled original, interesting and attractive, because it was impossible to call him handsome. Count Hasso had the height which, combined with the leanness often associated with it, produces a figure similar to Offenbach's Prince of Arcadia—a figure whose every garment seems borrowed, and hangs limp on the limbs. Every novelty in the fashion journals, even were it the most monstrous idea of some Paris or London brain, was first adopted by Count Raven, who liked to appear in society attired in the most extravagant elegance. His mouth was large, and frequently opened for a yawn, at which no one took offense; or for some witless remark intended to arouse a laugh, and which duly fulfilled its purpose. This mouth also opened at times to delight a circle of appreciative friends with a song, in a voice that certainly left much to be desired, but which had been trained by famous teachers in a series of the most expensive lessons, and elicited expressions of rapture on all sides. What did it matter if a false note occurred here and there? Count Raven sang it—and Count Raven was a good match.

Marie could never forget her first meeting with this hero of sporting circles.

Countess Raven had greeted her at the station, and conducted her to the room assigned for her use. She was expected in the dining-room at the tea hour, and meanwhile a maid, placed at her orders, was unpacking the young lady's trunks in the next room.

Marie went down to the countess's *boudoir* before the appointed hour, to spend the time in examining the well-filled book-shelves. She almost started at the sight of a gentleman—a stranger—clad in the most careless attire, who was reclining in a rocking-chair and puffing clouds of smoke through his nose.

"Pardon me! Come in, cousin!" he called, in a somewhat harsh accent, without changing his attitude in the least. "Excuse my negligee, but I've just come from some confoundedly tiresome races. My jockey was thrown, and I rode the second heat myself. Zounds! It was tremendously tiresome!

But, by the way, welcome to our house. I shouldn't have known you at all."

He put a pair of eye-glasses on his nose and, without altering his negligent posture, held out his hand. Marie took no notice of the gesture, but bowed somewhat formally, and said that she would not interrupt him longer. His boorish manners irritated her.

"*Bêtise!*" replied Hasso, soothingly. "You see, Marie, that I don't disturb myself at all—don't allow myself to be interrupted. I never do—never! You won't shake hands with me? Very well, just as you choose. I understand the timidity of you ladies. But no ceremony; draw up yonder chair and sit down. I'll read you a few capital jokes from *Punch*. I hope you understand English?" He pointed with his foot toward the piece of furniture. His morocco slipper fell off, displaying a red-silk stocking. "Miserable *canaille!*" cried Hasso, bending his noble back to replace it. He would doubtless have accepted the service had Marie sprung forward to relieve him of the trouble. "There are plenty of liveried rascals running about the house," he went on, trying to find the most comfortable place among the cushions. "They fairly tread on one another's heels; but nobody is at hand when wanted—of course!"

This sort of treatment began to amuse the young

baroness. She knew that she was dealing with an *enfant gaté*, and quietly took her seat in the chair designated, asking, with a suppressed laugh, whether tea was usually served so late.

Raven stretched himself.

"I really don't know, *ma belle*," he confessed, anxiously tying his Indian kerchief in the exact knot desired. "I very rarely take tea with mamma; these *tête-à-têtes* are so horribly wearisome, and we usually have guests only at dinners or evening entertainments; besides, I am so overwhelmed with invitations that I 'm often compelled to practice all sorts of tricks to escape these notes, even to get to the theatre. True, we don't have much in this hole. A few passable ballet-dancers. Pshaw! People here are very modest in their claims!" Count Hasso said all this in a tone as *blasé* as possible; then, leaning back again, stretched his legs before him and puffed out volumes of smoke. "Zounds! Did you notice that ring, cousin? Smokers make such a fad of such things now. There it is again. Capital! Perhaps you would like a cigarette, too?"

Marie declined; took up a book, and examined the fine illustrations.

"I remained at home to-day especially on your account," Hasso went on, scanning the young lady as if he expected at least a fainting fit in acknowledgment of such graciousness. "Mamma thought decorum demanded it. At first I was to go to the station for you, but, to be frank, cousin, you arrived at such an inconvenient hour that I could not possibly take out my bays again; they have done enough for to-day." He took a paper and some tobacco from an elegant case, twisted another cigarette, then settled himself comfortably to smoke.

Marie assured him that she had not expected such a sacrifice, and Hasso thought this quite a matter of course, then glanced at the clock and muttered an oath under his breath.

"Aren't you hungry, Marie? Nobody knows what they are all about to-day. It's half-past eight o'clock. But look here. I'm used to their tricks, and provide accordingly. Taste these conserved fruits. They are nice, I assure you. My dog and I eat a box of them every day. Minka has followed my taste very quickly. By the way, have you heard of my dogs? I'm passionately fond of training them. Minka leaps superbly. I'll show you the creatures some time, only please don't ask me this evening. I know by the young ladies here that they can never wait for me to begin. I'm too much used up to-day, 'pon honor." He slipped a bit of peach into his mouth, and again offered the box to the young lady. "I get these things direct from Sarotti," he added. "He knows my exacting taste and sends me nothing but first-class goods. I hope, cousin, that you will share some of my various pursuits. I shall be pleased to escort you to the theatre, concerts, etc., if it can be done without interfering with my usual engagements. It mustn't be any restraint upon me, *comprenez-vous?* Will mamma accompany us? Why, you see, cousin, my *petite maman* often promises a great deal which she does not and cannot perform. She is so much in demand. People fairly quarrel over us, and I am quite accustomed to make my bow to her empty chair. But that can be arranged. I just heard the hall-door open. She is coming at last."

He leaned his head back, and gazed wearily at the door.

"*Bon soir, maman!*" he said, without rising. "Excuse my keeping my seat. I'm fairly knocked up."

Countess Raven kissed his forehead as she passed.

"Good-evening, darling."

Then she held out her hand to Marie with a pleasant smile.

"Ah, so you have already made each other's acquaintance, children?" she cried, in her vivacious tones. "It is delightful to see how young people waive ceremony, and—yes, as unconcernedly as possible, my Hasso in a dressing-gown! But, *mon ange*, that is really too negligee for a first meeting."

She tapped his cheek lightly with her fan, then turned to the young baroness:

"Forgive him, Marie! He is often still a mere child, who hesitates at nothing. But I rejoice that he is still unspoiled. We so rarely find that among young men of the present day. You will be satisfied with him in other respects. My Hasso is considered a finished cavalier. He sings delightfully, is a very fair artist, and the ladies here go into raptures over him. Isn't that true, Hasso? And it doesn't make him the least bit vain. He is always the same—agreeable to every one. People envy me this son. Have you been talking long? It grew rather late. I had several letters to finish; but I hope tea has been brought to you?"

The young count had at last risen with a heavy sigh, and clattered on exaggeratedly high heels to the mirror.

"Count Hasso offered me some of his delicious fruit," said Marie, smiling. "He had so much of it that we were in no danger of starving."

"What? 'Count Hasso?' Surely, child, you will not address your cousin so formally?" cried the countess, in horror. "Why, that's an unheard-of thing. Come here, my dear; shake hands, and call each other 'thou,' as you ought."

"I've already offered her my hand, mamma," cried the heir of Raveneck; "but Marie would not take it. But I've treated her just like a cousin, though she was so distant."

"Yes, my Hasso becomes acquainted at once!" said his mother, smiling. "Come, my son, offer Marie your arm, and let us go to dinner."

* * * * * *

This was Marie's first impression of the young man, and, unfortunately, all the time of their intercourse could give no more attractive view of him. His exaggerated familiarity, especially in the presence of strangers, affected Marie almost unpleasantly. The hints of acquaintances, and even of Aunt Raven herself, which intimated that a future wedding was in prospect, seemed an absurdity to the young girl. But she maintained silence toward her aunt as well as to her mother, and merely treated the young hero to a few ready retorts, which reduced him to the condition of an embarrassed school-boy. Nevertheless, Count Hasso sometimes paid a visit to D——, and was thoroughly convinced of the honor he paid the gray old house by his august presence.

The baroness seemed to have expected the son of the clever Countess Raven to be a person very unlike this affected dandy, who had scarcely outgrown the childishness of youth. His immature character was by no means suited to attract or bestow lasting happiness upon a woman of earnest nature; and Baroness von Rotterswyl, seeing this only too plainly, decided, though with a heavy heart, to renounce her long-cherished desire to see Marie mistress of Castle Raveneck.

The old baroness was strangely changed since her return from Wiesbaden. Brand's end had made a far deeper impression upon her than any one would have imagined, and the pallid death-mask, which had lain at her feet, seemed to have reopened old wounds which were now no longer closed with icy pride, but permitted to bleed in mild, beneficent tears, shed upon the breast of her own child.

Marie scarcely recognized her mother. She could not understand this sudden revulsion of feeling, but she suspected that the hour had come which made the ice melt and the buds of love and tenderness in the heart unfold. The relation between the mother and the daughter grew warmer. They began to comprehend each other, and the baroness obtainted many a glimpse of her child's soul, which made her seriously consider how to drive the cloud from her brow. She read with more than usual interest the news of the army corps to which Gerrald belonged, and glanced with evident haste and anxiety over the list of the losses of the German officers.

Ascending the steps leading to the little bow-window room, she scarcely dared to enter the peaceful chamber from which rang the notes of Marie's gay song. The newspaper containing the mournful tidings rustled in her hand. She paused, then reluctantly crossed the threshold, gravely showed her daughter the news of Gerrald's wound, and uttered no reproof when the poor girl threw herself, sobbing, into her arms; nay, she even uttered a few words of sympathy for her young friend and hoped he would soon recover.

Ah, how this new gentleness from the proud woman comforted Marie!

So the months passed slowly away.

* * * * * *

It was a bright spring Sunday, clear and radiant with the fresh green leafage that appeared on every bush and shrub awakening to new life. The terrible cold of winter had passed away, and the crocuses and early primroses were already perfuming the warm air. Marie was knitting socks for the wounded men, and had just examined a heel with an air of satisfaction, when the door was hurriedly opened, and her maid, Liesbeth Lohfeld, almost rushed in.

"Pardon me, baroness," she cried, her cheeks glowing with an almost purple flush from her haste, "but I bring such good news that I ran all the way from the mills here in fifteen minutes. Just think, my Friedrich has been made corporal!"

"Good heavens!" said Marie, clasping her hands. "You have reason to be congratulated, Liesbeth. Fortune seems to favor Friedrich. He remains unhurt, and is promoted. I am very glad."

"And he writes, too, that he shall not go back to service after the campaign, but remain with the army," continued Lohfeld's daughter, joyously. "Then we can be married at once, and I shall be 'Mrs. Corporal,'" she added, with marked emphasis. "But here, *fräulein*, I have something for you, too," she whispered, mischievously, drawing a letter from her pocket. "As I met father, he called before I reached him: 'Liesel—Master Gerrald—'"

"What?" cried the young girl, starting up and trying to seize the letter. "From him?"

"Written to me," the little maid went on, mischievously holding the letter behind her; "he is much better, the fever has left him, and—"

"Show it to me—let me read it!" cried Marie, with flaming cheeks. And Liesbeth, with a beaming smile, gave her the letter.

"I knew it would please the baroness; that's why I brought it," she said, frankly.

Then, after watching her young lady hurriedly unfold the sheet and scan its contents, she turned and noiselessly left the room. She knew that people prefer to read such lines alone.

Marie read with a throbbing heart that he had

been seriously ill, but was now better. At present he was in the E—— hospital, but should return to his regiment as soon as possible; that the armistice would doubtless be followed by peace, and that it would give him infinite happiness to return home. And here at the end, in black and white—Marie read the passage twice—three times—were the words: "I hope Liesbeth is still in the service of the baroness. Ask her to remember me to both ladies, and present my greetings from the enemy's country. I trust all is well."

Yes, there it was, in large, distinct letters. She was not mistaken. So he thought of her, was convalescent, and perhaps would soon return? Ah, thou merciful Father in heaven, with how many tears of gratitude she offered thanks for this message of peace! Marie laughed and wept in the same breath, pressed the letter to her heart, and was on her way downstairs to her mother when Verja came to meet her, waving a newspaper aloft.

"Peace! Peace!" she cried, breathlessly. "Thank Heaven! Here is the dispatch."

The young girl stared at the lines; the printed letters danced before her eyes; she could not grasp the meaning of these blissful words.

"Rejoice, Marie!" exclaimed Verja, wild with delight. "Now, thank Heaven, they will all come home, and not a hair of Fritz's head is hurt! Out with your flag—quick! Every street is filled with banners! Do you hear? They are just ringing the bells, too! Hurrah!" And passing her arm around her niece's slender figure, she drew her to the window.

" Joy—nothing but joy to-day!" murmured Marie, with clasped hands, and for the first time the full significance of this message of peace came to her, with all the hopes following in its train. She rejoiced at the notes of the bells and the radiance of the spring, as she let the folds of her flag flutter under the blue sky. Peace!

CHAPTER XXII.

IN THE MILL.

"Look alive with your work!" ordered Inspector Lohfeld, swinging his hammer, with an eager glance around him. "Here, Josef, hand me up the fine needles; choose the thickest bunches, and bind them by twos, with young oak-leaves between or sprigs from yonder holly-tree. Zounds! This will be a splendid welcome!" And he again dealt a few vigorous blows to drive the nails through the green boughs on the door-posts; then, shading his eyes with his hand, he drew back to enjoy the whole effect. He scanned with evident satisfaction the gayly-painted shield bearing the inscription shining in the huge wreath. Lohfeld himself had wielded the brush to paint the "Welcome" for his young master. It was difficult work for the untrained fingers, but he finally accomplished it, and now the interlaced letters gazed down at him like a record of immortal fame.

The mills, adorned with gala decorations, awaited the coming of their lord and master, looking very unfamiliar in their festal splendor. On the sides of the entrance rose two slender masts, visible for a long distance, twined with gay garlands, between which were various coats of arms, while crossed banners fluttered proudly in the air. A thick garland of pine-needles united them like a waving triumphal arch, bearing in the center a shield, which was to greet the returning hero from the distance. Every door in the court-yard was twined with green; the German colors, blended with those of the country, floated from gables and attic windows, while tall oleanders and cedars were grouped in tasteful masses around steps and pillars.

Even the old well in the court-yard had assumed a holiday aspect; small pine-trees concealed its weather-beaten roof, and bright-hued paper roses decked it here and there amid the green boughs; two maid-servants still stood talking in front of it, while fastening the flowers in a few empty spaces.

Lohfeld had just shouted a word of cheer, then turning to his door again, he hammered away to his heart's content. The fuller and gayer of hue his decorations became, the greater grew the zeal of the worthy superintendent. Liesbeth was standing at the foot of the ladder, industriously handing up the golden bits of tinsel, while from time to time she surveyed the work with the air of a connoisseur, and finally asserted her entire satisfaction, though without every losing sight of the courtyard gate, through which Corporal Friedrich must pass if, faithful to his promise, he came there for a welcome.

Her young lady, too, as she had just told her father, had prepared to receive the troops. Marie von Rotterswyl held a magnificent laurel wreath, adorned with a blue ribbon, ready for the victors—or rather for one of them.

And now the hour had come, the fulfillment of many a fervent prayer and the hope of so many souls whose weal and woe were in Gerrald's hands. Hundreds of voices shouted a welcome from the depths of loyal hearts.

The adornment of the courtyard was completed. The workmen, men- and maid-servants stood in the center, and before the steps of the owner's residence, musicians were stationed on the steps themselves, and in front stood Inspector Lohfeld, with his wife and child; then, in the order of their rank, the rest of the principal employees.

All were in gala dress, with a little bunch of flowers on the breast or in the hat. Every face wore a happy smile, for each was animated by the same feeling, and full of gratitude to God for having restored a master whose equal it would have been hard to find.

The young man, who was honored by old and young with sincere love and devotion, had become their protector, their support, their father.

Lohfeld's eyes sparkled with pride and pleasure, as, raising his toil-hardened hand with an eager gesture, he explained once more the order to cheer.

"A thundering three-times three!" he exclaimed. "Let them hear it as far as the city, just as he reaches the entrance-gate, and when the carriage stops we'll all shout together: 'Long live Master Gerrald!' and I'll step forward and deliver the welcome. Liesbeth will hand him the bouquet, and we'll give another cheer—a good loud one! And you youngsters, up above, are to sound a flourish at the beginning and end, such as hasn't been heard in the city to-day! The best the brass can do; do you understand? Zounds, but our master shall hear that his millers are in earnest!"

Again he marched up and down like a general surveying his faithful troops.

Just at that moment a boy at the gate shouted at the top of his voice:

"Look out! Here he comes, and two others with him!"

The news flashed through the waiting throng like an electric spark. The men fell into position, and Lohfeld loosened his collar and rubbed his hands in anticipation of what was coming. The flags on the masts fluttered, as though waving an impatient greeting, the sun laughed from the blue sky upon the green leaves, and a thundering "Hurrah!" thrice repeated, welcomed the handsome officer dashing on his fiery steed through the open gate.

He paused before the steps and waved a salute with his glittering sword; but the shouts of joy drowned his words, and, forgetting rules and order, the crowd poured forward, surrounding horse and rider like the waves of the sea.

Had Gerrald possessed a hundred arms, they would not have sufficed to extend to all the hands outstretched in greeting as the men pressed eagerly forward to hold the young officer's stirrup.

"Liesbeth," cried Lohfeld, suddenly, grasping his daughter's arm, "the master is wearing your baroness's laurel wreath!"

And he pointed excitedly to the green garland which hung around the officer's neck, and whose blue ribbons twined treacherously across his breast.

Liesbeth gazed at it with clasped hands. Her little face beamed brightly, and forgetting everything around her, she joyously exclaimed:

"Hurrah! Then it was made for him!" and with a happy expression, she offered her bouquet. "Welcome, Master Traugott!"

CHAPTER XXIII.

AN INTERLUDE.

Aunt Verja was standing beside Marie, examining the blue-bells in the young baroness's golden hair.

"Very pretty, *petite!*" she nodded, gayly. "You will look like the personification of woodland poesy in that wreath. I'll fasten it for you myself, so that every little blossom will show. Sit down, little Alseide, and arrange the mirror conveniently for me. Was it your own idea to wear a wreath of oak leaves and forest flowers to welcome our brave soldiers?"

Marie glanced up into the Russian's beautiful face, and answered, smiling:

"What could a German girl choose that would be more fitting than the colors of her home? I think she can also wear them in the ball-room. Do you suppose Herr Gerrald will be there, aunt?"

She was handing her a hair-pin, and Verja noticed how the little white hand trembled.

"I hope so! I should be very sorry not to see him in his uniform. I should like to make the young hero a little vain, and tell him that it is very becoming. There, will you have this spray fastened closer, or leave it loose?"

Verja leaned back and looked at her niece's little head. She was satisfied.

Just at that moment some one tapped lightly at the door, and the maid noiselessly entered.

"Count Raven has just arrived from Frankfort, and my mistress begs the ladies to come down as soon as possible."

Baroness von Kartegg adjusted the glittering gold bracelet on her arm and stepped in front of the mirror.

"We'll come directly, as soon as Fräulein Marie is ready."

She stooped to arrange the pink-silk folds of her train.

"Good heavens! Count Raven!" cried Marie, in horror, as the door closed behind the girl. "What does he want now, especially this evening, when he knows that we are to attend the officers' ball?"

"Tell me, Marie, can you really endure Count Raven?" asked Verja, suddenly planting herself before the young baroness, with the gaze of an inquisitor. "Tell me frankly and honestly; I want to know the truth."

"No, aunt—certainly not!" Marie declared, so promptly and sincerely that no doubt was possible.

"Thank God!" said the Russian, with a sigh of relief. "He is the very last person whom I should have desired for a nephew. But now let us hurry down, *chérie*. I'm famishing for candied fruit." And, laughing merrily, she took the blue and silver gauze from the chair to wrap the young girl in its misty folds.

Meanwhile, "my son Hasso" was pacing from one mirror to another in the green drawing-room below, sometimes scrutinizing his patent-leather shoes and sometimes twisting his elegant silk handkerchief, which was strongly scented with Flang-Flang, around his hands.

Baroness von Rotterswyl sat silently on her chair, smoothing the fingers of her light kid gloves, and occasionally casting a swift glance at the young dandy, who now stopped before the piano, opened it, and took his seat, with his limbs stretched in front of him.

"Oh, a song!" The old lady took her fan and lace handkerchief from her lap and laid it on the inlaid table at her side. "I have never heard you sing, Hasso."

"Sing? To night?" replied the count, throwing back his head, as if considering the matter. "Really, aunt, I'm not capable of it before a ball.

I need repose, mood, inspiration for my performances, and I've travelled by rail to-day from Frankfort to D——. No, aunt, I can't sing. I would rather play." And he began to rattle out of time the notes of a polka.

A smile difficult to interpret hovered around the lips of the baroness; the most bitter irony, mingled with a faint, sorrowful regret, as though she were bidding farewell to a beautiful dream.

The *portières* softly parted, and Verja's radiant figure glided in, holding her handkerchief to her lips and imitating the swaying movements of the pianist, whose performance crimsoned her cheeks with suppressed laughter.

Baroness von Rotterswyl shook her head and turned to glance at Marie, who stood slender and fair as a silvery cloud in the dark velvet framework of the *portières*. She exchanged a mischievous glance with Verja, and then threw her beautiful arm tenderly around the old lady's neck, pressing a loving kiss upon her cheek.

Just at that instant Count Raven struck a few bold chords, let his outspread hands rest on the keys a moment, then rose with the weary, absent smile with which great artists are prone to respond to the plaudits of a crowded concert hall.

"Bravo, Count Raven!" cried Verja, rolling up her eyes with simulated rapture. "Who would have dreamed of experiencing such a pleasure so late in the evening? You play bewitchingly—a marvelously beautiful performance."

Marie pressed her handkerchief to her lips to hide her laugh by turning it into a cough. Her mother cast a glance of alarm at Verja, whose eyes sparkled with mischief; but Count Raven, perfectly assured that the praise was sincere, bowed graciously to the ladies.

"Good evening, madam. I kiss your little hand, dear cousin! Yes, yes, I knew that my polka would please you! The young ladies in Frankfort are fairly bewitched with this piece, and rarely let an entertainment pass without persuading me to go to the piano! So you are in full ball-dress? Superb, ladies, superb!" and with evident good humor, the heir of Raveneck put on his eye-glasses and scanned the elegant costumes.

"But you, too, are dressed as though you intended to break hearts in the first waltz, Count Raven." Verja held her open fan before the laughing face. "Do you intend to accompany us to celebrate your cruel triumphs in our peaceful capital?"

"I really meant to surprise you, ladies, by appearing in the ball-room to request a dance; but it was so horribly tiresome in the hotel, with nothing but lieutenants and waiters, that I determined to come here."

"Extremely flattering!" the Russian protested; and Marie asked gravely why Count Hasso had not come in the morning to witness the imposing entry of the troops?

With what often seemed malicious enthusiasm, she spoke of the brave fellows who had left their homes, wives, children and property to devote their lives to the service of their native land! She had scattered flowers and laurels in their path, and thrown garlands to the heroes whose breasts were adorned with the cross. Meanwhile, Count Hasso had sat at home, training dogs and playing the polka to young ladies.

Verja turned to the baroness; her bright face had grown strangely earnest.

"Did you see Herr Gerrald among the officers?" she asked. "He wears the iron cross."

"Because he has fought like a hero," answered the widowed noblewoman, in a very harsh tone. "He has proved that the blue blood of the Rotterswyl race flows in the veins of this Prince of the Mill also. Count Raven," she turned with her head held haughtily erect, "give me your arm, the carriage has driven up."

The servant put on the ladies' cloaks, and Count Hasso obediently led the way with the baroness.

"My husband will receive us as a member of the ball committee," whispered Verja, joyously. "Just think, Marie, I shall dance half the sets with Fritz to-night. I shall be jealous of him, he looks so handsome with the long beard he grew during the campaign!"

Marie followed as though in a dream, trembling at the thought of the happiness of this first meeting. What torture it would be to utter formal words of welcome in the presence of the multitude!

* * * * * *

The spacious ball-room resembled an ocean of light and splendor, through whose countless flames waved the joy-banner of peace. From the vaulted ceiling garlands and slender green boughs twined around pillars and pilasters, fastened by escutcheons and military emblems, above which fluttered the colors of united Germany, while white marble busts of heroes, throned on pedestals, were surrounded by the names of the victories which had rendered them immortal in the book of fame.

Uniforms of every variety mingled in motly confusion. Bearded faces, before whose eyes so short a time ago war had unrolled its pictures of horror and despair, and whose gaze now rested upon the fairest shield of domestic happiness, the smiling faces of German maidens.

Near the door, tall, haughty and handsome as the statue of Mars above him, waving his glittering sword amid the green leafage, stood a young officer of hussars, who was frequently accosted and besieged with friendly questions.

At last she arrived. A burning flush crimsoned his face as, standing motionless among the group of fir-trees, he gazed at her lovely features. Yes, it was she—unchanged in beauty and grace—Marie.

The ladies were instantly surrounded. He timidly approached and bowed respectfully to Baroness von Rotterswyl, who held out her hand and welcomed him with sincere pleasure. Traugott scarcely recognized this gentle, cordial woman, whose lips wore a strangely sweet expression, and whose hair had suddenly turned white.

Then Gerrald addressed Verja, and at last reached Marie. A crowd surrounded her, and he could not utter indifferent words, but his eyes revealed the passionate emotions with which his heart seemed bursting.

"May I ask you for a dance, baroness?

Marie looked up, and he read in her blue eyes all the faithful, unfaltering love, all her anxiety and grief for her imperiled friend, all the rapturous joy of the meeting.

He asked for the first and last dance, then was obliged to draw back and make room for his comrades, who, with many compliments, were begging for the young lady's dancing card.

Count Hasso also requested it.

"The german already engaged?" he asked, in astonishment. "Why didn't you keep that for me, cousin?"

"Because you did not ask me to do so, count," replied Marie, laughing.

"Gerrald? Is the name Gerrald?" said the heir of Raveneck. "*Von* Gerrald?"

Marie frowned.

"No—Herr Gerrald," she said, curtly.

"Ah, yes, I remember. That's the mysterious Prince of the Mill with whom all the ladies are said to be in love." He laughed loudly. "I hope you don't mean to dance the german with this insignificant merchant, Marie?"

"Herr Gerrald invited me for the german, so I shall dance it with him."

"A pretty business! So I've come all the way from Frankfort to see you dance with a Herr Gerrald! I supposed you would naturally reserve it for me. I never make engagements in advance. It confines people, and is sometimes annoying afterward. By the way, I rarely dance the german at all. Ladies are too ready to imagine all sorts of things; but I would have risked it with you, Marie. You are my cousin, and what you may be some day—" He half shut his eyes and shrugged his shoulders significantly. "Oh, pshaw! Let this

Herr Gerrald drop. You know you regret your promise. Where is this miller-hero?"

"I am ready, Herr Gerrald," said Marie, at the same moment, smiling up at a hussar officer, who silently bowed to her, and, without vouchsafing the bewildered count another glance, she entered the ball-room leaning on her partner's arm.

"Hail, Thou Who Victory's Laurels Wearest" sounded like a burst of exultation from the hidden orchestra.

"Aha! So that's the fellow!" thought Count Hasso, opening his eyes to their widest extent. "I'll settle the miller!" And turning abruptly to the right, he crossed the hall to inspect the richly furnished sideboard in the adjoining room. Meanwhile Traugott and Marie were dancing the polonaise. The music was loud and noisy; the surging sea of human beings around them laughed and talked till the sound resembled the buzzing of a hive of bees. Gerrald bent low toward Marie.

"Have you not a single word of welcome for me?" he asked in an agitated tone. "Was the green laurel wreath flung from the distance your only language for the returning soldier?"

She looked him full in the eyes. "I know no words which can express such a wealth of heartfelt joy and gratitude," she said simply.

"Then you have held me in remembrance, Marie,

have cherished your pure, sacred love for me, which I had believed forfeited and hoped to regain in death?" he whispered with passionate fervor. "I had imagined a different meeting—not here in this noisy, glittering ball-room, surrounded by thousands of curious eyes and ears. My first visit was to be to you and your mother, Marie, from whom I desired to ask my greatest earthly happiness!"

Her only answer was a look. The dance separated her a moment from her lover, and she moved smiling, with bent head, as if in a dream, in the line of brilliantly dressed ladies.

Figure followed figure; acquaintances addressed Marie in jesting words; Gerrald often shook a comrade's proffered hand as they passed in the dance. It was impossible to talk and express the emotions of their overflowing hearts, as they mutely moved in the glittering train, which seemed to float on the jubilant melody of the National Hymn. At last the graceful tangle separated, the music melted into the notes of a waltz and, like a cloud of butterflies, the couples hovered over the smooth floor.

Traugott led his partner back to her mother, who inquired about his long illness and his present state of health, the horrors of the war, and the period of suffering in the hospital; and when Marie was claimed by another partner, the handsome officer took the seat she had vacated beside the old lady, and in his deep, musical tones, described his experiences, the bloody battle-field and the meeting with Heloise. A shiver ran through the limbs of the listener, and her face blanched.

Question followed question, until the young man's white brow crimsoned, as his companion's proud lips congratulated him on the cross that decked his breast.

Meanwhile, Count Raven strolled through the hall with a very weary look; he had danced an extra waltz with the daughter of the Austrian ambassador, a vivacious little blonde, whose acquaintance he had made in his mother's house at Frankfort. Now he scanned the ladies through his eye-glasses with an air of the utmost unconcern, and then gazed about in search of Herr Gerrald, with whom he meant to settle the business of the german. Just at that moment he saw the person of whom he was in quest take leave of Baroness von Rotterswyl and go to one of the open windows, where he stood looking out into the mild spring night.

The heir of Raveneck determined not to miss the opportunity, and, crossing the hall, stood the next instant beside the young officer, whose slender figure towered so far above him that he scarcely reached his shoulder.

"Excuse me, sir; you are Herr Gerrald, if I am

not mistaken?" he said, with a patronizing nod. "I am Count Raven—Raveneck."

Traugott bowed.

"To what do I owe the honor?" he asked, eying the boyish young dandy with evident surprise.

"You engaged my cousin, Fräulein von Rotterswyl, for the german," Hasso went on, in a drawling tone. He had wiped his eye-glasses with his handkerchief, and again placed them on his nose to scan the young hussar from head to foot. "I have come to settle the matter."

Traugott could not trust his ears.

"Settle the matter?" he repeated, doubtfully, his face darkening under the count's impertinent gaze. "Fräulein von Rotterswyl knows that I engaged her, and I do not think there can be any confusion, as I have invited no other lady."

Count Raven smiled, and nonchalantly twisted the little bunch of violets in his fingers.

"That's just it, my dear sir," he said, over his shoulder. "My cousin, unfortunately, is aware that, in her haste, she promised a dance which—well, which she would have preferred to have given to some one else!"

He uttered a short laugh and ground the high heel of his shoe into the smooth floor.

Traugott stood facing him, with his face blanched to a ghostly pallor and his tall figure drawn to its full height, while his chest heaved with his laboring breath.

"And what do you desire of me, Count Raven?" His voice sounded icy cold, and his features looked as though they were carved from stone.

"Dear me, surely you understand!" said Hasso, nervously. "Must everything be told down to the most minute detail? My cousin requests you to release her from her promise—*voilà tout!*"

"Did Fräulein von Rotterswyl herself send you here with this message?"

Gerrald did not stir, but his eyes blazed with the most intense excitement.

Raven flung the violets out of the window with studied carelessness; then, shrugging his shoulders, cast an insolent glance at Gerrald.

"You seem very hard to convince, sir. I should think it would not be so incomprehensible that a young lady had changed her mind—*femme rare*, as the French say. Surely you must know that best, as you came directly from France."

A look of unspeakable scorn rested upon the frivolous speaker.

"Then Fräulein von Rotterswyl prefers to dance with *you?*"

Traugott's lips curled with the most bitter sarcasm. He felt an impulse to laugh aloud in his rage and grief; and yet no, it was impossible. Marie could never have inflicted such a slight upon him. He did not hear the count's conceited "Certainly ;" but, with a hasty step forward, stood at his side, saying, curtly :

"Follow me, Count Raven. I am sorry to be compelled to say that I must have Fräulein von Rotterswyl's confirmation of your statement."

He led the way, and Count Hasso, biting his lips, followed, muttering :

"Such a fuss about nothing !"

Marie stood talking eagerly with an elderly officer, close beside the group of fir-trees, overtopped by blossoming oleanders and laurestinas, which concealed the band of musicians.

Marie had rested her arm on the bronze pedestal of a Germania; her hand, lightly grasping a glittering fan, was relieved against the metal background, and her smiling face, flushed by the exercise of dancing and animated by her large blue eyes, was raised to the bearded colonel as earnestly as if she longed to read his very thoughts ere his lips uttered them.

Gerrald advanced and bowed formally to the speaker. His brow was dark and grave, and the glance which rested on the young girl's face seemed almost unfriendly.

"Pardon me, baroness. Count Raven has just been to see me, and I have come in person—to hand you my dancing-card, which is now useless."

"Don't forget the Grand Cross in the german, *fräulein!*" said the colonel, jestingly, as he took leave. "I am proudly anticipating the honor. Good evening, gentlemen."

Marie turned to Traugott with questioning eyes.

"Your dancing-card?" she repeated, shaking her head. "What am I to do with it?"

"Erase your name from the german, as you desired." He spoke quietly, but his eyes rested steadily on her sweet face.

"My name! Don't you wish to dance with me?" She looked up almost terrified. "Good heavens, what has happened?"

No, those sweet lips could not lie! A burning blush crimsoned Gerrald's brow. He hastily moved a step nearer and asked:

"Then you did not send Count Raven?"

Marie, her lovely face suddenly paling, turned to the young dandy, who was unconcernedly breaking off the green needles of the firs.

"Count Hasso," she said, sternly, "there seems to be some misunderstanding here. Will you please explain?"

"My little cousin," replied the nobleman, "you look like a judge sentencing a criminal. It's really absurd to make such a talk over the trifle. Tell Herr Gerrald yourself that you prefer to dance with me;" and half turning, he gazed after the little

Austrian, who had given him a languishing glance as she danced past him.

Marie looked hopelessly at Gerrald.

"I don't understand," she said, clasping her hands anxiously. "Tell me, Herr Gerrald, what does all this mean?"

A radiant smile brightened the face of the young mill-owner.

"I see that there must be some mistake here," he said, with quickened breath. "Count Raven came to me and asked, in your name, a release from the engagement to dance the german, which you had given too hastily. So that was not true? You did not send your cousin?"

"Good heavens!" she exclaimed, in horror. "I knew nothing at all about it." And trembling with indignation, she turned to Count Hasso. "How could you have made such a mistake? How did you venture to arrange in my name matters concerning which I never had a thought of consulting you?"

Hasso threw back his head and measured Gerrald with a look of the most insulting arrogance.

"Because, Marie, I might suppose that you would prefer to dance with Count Raven rather than with Herr Gerrald, the mill-owner."

And tearing a handful of green needles from one of the trees, he tossed it scornfully on the shining floor.

The tall, proud figure of the officer of hussars confronted him. The cross of honor glittered on his breast, and the blue vein swelled on his forehead.

"Enough, sir," he said, with crushing dignity. "You will permit me to give my answer to that remark when we are alone." Then turning to Marie, he added, with a sudden change of tone: "*Au revoir!* I will not resign my claim to the german."

"Alone? That is a challenge!" exclaimed Raven, barring his way, while his characterless face expressed the utmost embarrassment. "A duel? Ah, charming—charming! Ha! ha! ha! Listen, cousin. I am to risk my life for your sake," and again he uttered a laugh so loud and forced that Gerrald, with the utmost contempt, turned his back upon him.

"I did not imagine, Count Raven, that you possessed so little tact as to discuss such subjects in the presence of ladies."

"Merciful God!" pleaded Marie, white as the marble statue at her side. "You won't take the affair so seriously, Herr Gerrald? Oh, tell me that you will not challenge him!" Approaching with clasped hands, she gazed with mortal terror into his gloomy eyes. "Traugott!" she said, softly. "Traugott!"

"Don't trouble yourself about it, Marie. The

whole affair is absurd!" cried the heir of Raveneck, in a shrill tone. "Farewell, cousin. It's a mere *bagatelle*," and tossing his head, he turned on his heel, and walked carelessly to one of the adjacent rooms. He had plenty of friends whose finances were always at a low ebb, who would consider it an honor to fight for the aristocratic favorite of the Frankfort society dames. Gold rules the world, was the thought with which Count Raven consoled himself.

Traugott gazed earnestly at Marie's terrified face and, leading her to a divan, he sat down by her side.

"Do you really expect me to let that arrogant boy's insult pass unpunished?" he asked quietly "I owe it to this uniform to let no speck sully its lustre."

"You yourself call the count a boy, and yet wish to judge him as a man!" she exclaimed wildly. "Oh, I will not suffer you to risk your life again after escaping, as if by a miracle, from all the perils of war! Oh, no; promise, promise me to keep the peace. I cannot endure the thought of being the cause of this unhappy quarrel."

Tears sparkled in her eyes, and her voice was full of heart-rending entreaty.

Gerrald, smiling, tried to soothe her.

"The count must beg my pardon," he said, "and,

so far as I can judge, I am quite sure that he will."

Just at that moment a lieutenant of dragoons, who had been searching all through the hall for Marie, approached to claim his partner for the Lancers.

"He must ask your pardon; that is the only way to appease you," whispered the young girl, hurriedly. And as Traugott bent his proud head in assent, she rose with a faint glimmer of satisfaction on her pale face.

"Pardon me, baroness," said the dragoon, his spurs clanking as he bowed before her. "I've been searching for you all through the hall. The crowd is tremendous. Excuse me for taking away your lady, Gerrald!" And he slipped Marie's hand through his arm, and led her swiftly to their place in the Lancers.

How slowly the minutes passed! The dance seemed endless. At last, at last, her partner again offered his arm, and, with an expression of thanks, led her back to her seat. Marie cast a hasty glance around the hall, and saw Count Hasso standing beside the fragrant orange-trees, and before him, half hidden by a group of palms, was the coquettish little Austrian, laughing and flirting, the one thought in her pretty head being that the man before her was a good match.

Marie drew nearer. The heir of Raveneck was offering his box of fruits, and, with his mouth full, describing how one of his trained dogs had just gone lame in the left hind paw.

"Aha, little cousin," he interrupted, "you must have seen my box in the distance; there is an apricot on top, just as sweet and rosy as yourself!" And laughing loudly at his own gallantry, he proffered the *bonbonnière*.

"Adieu, Count Raveneck!" said the ambassador's daughter, tossing her head, turning up her little nose, and abruptly greeting another partner who approached the young lady with a low bow.

"You see she took offense because I made you a lover-like speech!" said Hasso, with great amusement. "Ha! ha! little Bella thought she had me in her pocket."

A shade of displeasure clouded Marie's brow. She declined the fruit, and said, hastily:

"Listen to me a moment, Count Hasso. I want to speak seriously."

"Very well. I suppose it's about the duel. Ha, ha, ha! Let me have the fun of giving Herr Gerrald an aristocratic bullet as a souvenir!"

"Herr Gerrald has the reputation of being an excellent shot," whispered Marie, with a throbbing heart. "Perhaps it might be you, and not he, who would be the victim, Count Hasso; and then think of the despair of your poor mother and my own suffering for having been the cause of this misfortune."

The young dandy threw back his chest, smiling.

"Would you weep and mourn for me all your life?" he asked cruelly.

Marie drew farther back behind the green boughs.

"Oh, do not jest about such things," she cried, skillfully evading the difficult question; "think rather of how to save yourself for the world and your friends! Why conjure up the bloody scene which may have consequences so serious for you, Count Hasso!" and she raised her clasped hands beseechingly. "I entreat you to relieve my anxiety and be reconciled to Herr Gerrald."

"If it will relieve you, certainly!" replied Count Raven, in the blissful hope of having found a plausible motive for arranging the disagreeable business; "but I don't know how it is to be done."

Marie's eyes sparkled.

"Oh, there is nothing easier!" she cried eagerly. "Go with me to Herr Gerrald, and tell him that you would be sorry to be misunderstood, as you had not the slightest intention of offending him."

"H'm, that might do!" said Hasso, laughing pleasantly. "He did entirely misunderstand me. The whole affair was a mistake, which he took in the wrong way! But, of course, I must tell him all this alone—*vous comprenez, cousine?* On account of gossip!" He twirled his box of confectionery in his hands, keeping time with his foot to the gay polka performed by the orchestra.

"Then come quick; I'll take you to Herr Gerrald," urged Marie, in an agitated tone. And Hasso obediently offered his arm and escorted her through the hall.

A pair of eyes, flashing with anger, followed them. Then the fair-haired Austrian laughed and gave her delighted partner a rose-bud from her bouquet.

Gerrald was still sitting on the red-cushioned divan behind the group of fir-trees. His head rested against the wall, and his eyes were fixed on the huge eagle, with outspread wings, which held the green garlands in its beak. Hasty steps approached, and, like a vision in a dream, Marie stood before him, followed by his enemy, Count Raven.

"Herr Gerrald!" said Marie, with panting breath. "Count Raven is seeking you to express his regret for the misunderstanding, which was not intended to convey offense to you."

"Yes, I am sorry. It was a little jest," Raven added with a stupid smile. "I did not intend to vex you. Let us think no more about it. My cousin is frantic," and with a cordial "Shake!" he held out his gloved right hand to Gerrald,

Gerrald did not seem to see the gesture. He had risen and stood before the young man with an air of haughty reserve.

"You apologize for your want of tact?" he asked, in a sharp, curt tone.

"Yes, yes!" said Marie, hastily, and Count Hasso bowed his head in assent.

"Quite right," he said, in a tone of mingled embarrassment and discomfort.

"I am satisfied with your explanation," said Traugott, after a brief pause. A glance at Marie's blanched face calmed the angry excitement which the count's absurd behavior aroused, and turning from him, he bowed to the young girl. "I hope you are satisfied, baroness."

He did not vouchsafe the hero of Frankfort drawing-rooms another glance.

"Then everything is settled?" Hasso uttered a sigh of relief. "But in arranging this affair we have entirely forgotten to dance. This is my polka, cousin."

A flush of joy crimsoned Marie's cheeks.

"I thank you, Herr Gerrald," she murmured from the very depths of her heart, and then accompanied her impatient partner into the surging human sea which filled the ball-room.

The german was drawing to a close. Gerrald brought his partner the fragrant little bouquet, and

Marie, with sparkling eyes, fastened the order on his breast. The countless lights in the chandelier glittered above them, while the sounds and scents around them seemed like the joyous greeting of peace.

"And I may come to-morrow?" asked Traugott, with beaming eyes. He led his partner back to her mother. "May I say 'till we meet again?'"

Then a pair of blue eyes smiled at him, and rosy lips whispered:

"Till we meet again."

Count Hasso hastily swallowed a glass of champagne, and leaned thoughtfully against the sideboard.

"This paying court is a risky matter," he thought. "I'll end it to-morrow. The poor girl suffered terrible anxiety about me to-night, and trembled for my life. Well, she shall be rewarded."

This was Count Hasso's resolve

CHAPTER XXIV.

HAPPINESS AND REALIZATION.

Count Hasso sprang into the carriage and drove off, without vouchsafing the venerable gray house another glance, but sat propping his chin on the gold head of his cane in silent wonder, trying to understand this ninth marvel of the world—this fact which required much pondering to grasp. He, the heir of Castle Raveneck, the irresistible mortal for whom the Frankfort ladies were ready to go through fire, this breaker of hearts and peerless singer, the wearer of a coronet with nine points, this much-desired, courted and admired Count Raven, had—been rejected!

It was almost inconceivable ; and, yes, it was not quite clear to himself. He did not exactly believe it. And who gave this mitten? An insignificant little baroness, who positively had nothing at all except an aristocratic name and a pretty face. The few thousands of her fortune would barely furnish a man like Hasso with pocket-money; and who lived in a house—the rejected suitor threw back his head and turned up his nose—which was almost devoured by wood-worms, and might be expected to fall clattering about the occupants' heads at any moment. He would not have expected his groom to live in such an antiquated abode.

Bah! It was merely an evidence of alarming narrow-mindedness, inconceivable folly, which could only awaken pity, and, at last, become actually amusing from the rarity of having the hand of a Count Raven refused.

The jest would excite mirth in the circle of his intimate friends; they would laugh and congratulate the young man upon having escaped the consequences of childish haste so easily. Or would it be better for him to pass over the matter in total silence? But, no; she might boast of her triumph, and it would be better to take the initiative!

Hasso angrily pulled the photograph of the coy lady out of his pocketbook, and gazed at the lovely features with a frowning brow. "But the little witch *is* pretty!" he confessed defiantly. "Confound it! The very first time I have really fallen in love, to have such a—" The sentence ended in a sarcastic laugh.

"What will mamma say to it? She'll be amazed,

consider it ridiculous—absurd. And here these mischievous eyes look at me as though they wanted to laugh at my discomfiture! Deuce take them!" The heir of Raveneck tore the picture of his lost love, and threw himself back among the cushions. "Come, we'll forget!" he grumbled.

His box of candied fruit awakened other thoughts, and, opening it, he thoughtfully bit into a tempting apricot. But either, for the first time, the fruit was poor, or it was his own mood—at any rate, the beautiful apricot tasted bitter.

Meanwhile Marie von Rotterswyl was standing in her tower-room, pressing her burning brow against the panes. Her temples beat and throbbed so wildly, and her little heart seemed as if it were ready to burst its narrow confines and fly exultingly to meet "him." The room was so sultry, so oppressive. She opened the door and ran down into the garden, into the wide, surging sea of the fresh spring air, beneath the radiant sky, past the marble statues, by the yew hedge, till at last she stood by the little pond.

How still it was here! The turf was glittering with the first green of May; fresh, waving blades of grass, amid which bloomed the white stars of the daisy and early primroses. Hidden far beneath, too, were the sweet violets, which sent forth their fragrance on the soft breeze to greet her.

Marie sat down upon a log, and dreamed under the whispering boughs, whose silvery catkins drooped low over the quiet pool. The rusty chain for mooring boats lay at her feet, winding over the crumbling marble steps down into the mysterious depths. The yellow leaves of last year's rushes bowed rustling under the hem of her light-blue dress, which floated around her like an airy cloud.

It was a fair picture, the slender, girlish figure beside the neglected pond, the brown water-grasses nodding about her. She looked like a thoughtful nymph, who had just risen from the glittering spray.

How much the curious wrens on the willow-boughs would have liked to know what important thoughts occupied the fair little head, why the mouth smiled so bewitchingly, and the eyes were raised heavenward so thoughtfully, as if the radiant sunshine contained some vast, vast enigma, whose solution the young girl could not grasp!

Count Hasso had called a few hours before, and, with a very important air, requested to see Baroness von Rotterswyl.

Marie did not long for his society, especially to-day. When she was momentarily expecting the coming of another, who absorbed her every thought, and whose image alone hovered before her eyes— a tall, handsome officer, whose face grew radiant as he reined in his charger, to catch a wreath which floated down to him with fluttering ribbons. Ah, it was already four and twenty hours since she had seen him for the first time after their long separation. What a flood of thoughts filled her soul, what a longing contracted her heart, when she saw Verja rush so joyously into her husband's arms! She could rejoice before the world; could express her happiness in a thousand tender words, while Marie still stood at the window, gazing intently with tearful eye at the spot where "he" had just bowed his thanks for her greeting of love.

Ah, what would happen now! Will no sun of happiness ever rise? Yet she was full of hope. Her heart was overflowing with gratitude to God, who had permitted his return home. He lives, he loves you; do not despair, my heart.

She had been sitting in her little room, thinking of him alone. Then her mother entered, grave and solemn, as if she were come in the name of the law.

"Marie," she said, abruptly, "Count Raven asks your hand in marriage. Will you give it to him?"

Alas, it seemed as if a violent blow had shattered her sweet dream! What answer her cry of terror, her deadly fright made she knew not; she saw only the strange tremor of the old baroness's lips as she gravely stooped to kiss her on the forehead.

"And why do you refuse the count's hand?" she asked.

Then the ardent love in the young girl's heart no longer knew timidity or fear. Like a deep, long hidden fountain, which at last bursts all barriers and rises to the light of day, the confession poured from her lips, swifter, more jubilant, culminating in the rapturous avowal: "I love *him* alone!" And when the bonds were once broken, the seal removed from the timid lips, the shrinking child had no further thought of silence. Everything must be confessed, everything must ring in her mother's ears; and Baroness von Rotterswyl listened with an aching heart to this sacred, long-repressed fervor of first love—this suffering and hoping, fearing and yearning, and mortal dread of her mother's anger. And as her child's arms clasped her neck so tenderly, as every word found an answering chord in her own heart, and long-buried memories of her youth awoke, the very last barrier of pride melted, the ice of the proud soul thawed under the fire of love which poured so resistlessly from the lips of her child. She clasped her hands in a swift battle with herself; her tearful eyes wandered toward heaven, as though she were bidding farewell to a long-cherished dream; then she clasped her daughter to her heart in benediction, murmuring a short, almost incredible reply—that she should become the wife of the man she loved. And ere Marie could utter a word of gratitude, her mother's tall figure had vanished behind the door to give the waiting suitor her answer. Even now the baroness would not yield, could not let the mask fall so suddenly and reveal the unhappy, broken-hearted woman, whose whole life had been only a shield to hide the deep wounds dealt by love.

Marie stood alone, dazzled, almost giddy in the presence of the glow of happiness which had so suddenly followed her suffering.

Now she sat beside the pool, pondering.

Meanwhile Liesbeth stood at the door of the house, gazing down the street. Suddenly she shaded her eyes with her hand and bent forward. An officer of hussars was striding swiftly over the pavement, his spurs clanking as he moved. The maid recognized the tall figure and knew his errand.

"How do you do, Master Gerrald?" she said, courtesying.

"Liesbeth," he asked, his face flushing, "is Frau von Rotterswyl upstairs?"

"In the drawing-room," she answered.

"And Baroness Marie?"

"Alone in the garden," was the almost mischievous answer.

The young officer crimsoned to the brow.

"Liesbeth," he said, hastily, "I once did you a favor, and asked your father to let you go to the city. You told me, when you went away, that if you could ever render me a service in return, you would be ready. Do you remember? I will hold you to-day to your promise. Show me to the garden; make the mistake of supposing that *both* the ladies were there—"

"I understand, Herr Gerrald," Lohfeld's daughter nodded, gravely. "Follow me, please."

She passed through the corridor and led the young man across the courtyard into the garden.

The gravel creaked under Traugott's rapid footsteps, his saber rattled and his spurs rang on the stones, but not a word was exchanged between them. Suddenly Liesbeth paused and cast a searching glance around.

"I don't know where she can be," she said. "She isn't in the arbor; she very seldom goes to the linden walk. But stop; she is probably sitting by the pond. This way, please, Herr Gerrald. Yes, I see her blue dress yonder through the willow boughs. Keep straight on along this path. It will lead you there."

"Many thanks, Liesbeth," stammered Traugott, evidently trying to control his embarrassment. "I only want to speak to Baroness Marie. We'll come directly; but I would rather you did not announce me to Baroness von Rotterswyl just yet. Many thanks, Liesbeth; you 're a good girl." And he walked hastily away as if to escape the incredulous look with which the " good girl " greeted his " we 'll come directly." But Liesbeth was discreet, and only said, with a ludicrously solemn expression :

" Very glad to do it, Herr Gerrald," turned on her heel and fairly ran back to the house.

" Friedrich," she giggled to her approaching lover, " the 'pop' is coming." And when he asked the names and other particulars, she laid her finger mysteriously on her lips and murmured, " 'St !"

* * * * * *

The rushes were whispering their monotonous song around the dreaming girl, the birds on the willow-branch were singing low, sweet notes, and the outlines of the fair face quivered on the water, melting into its own golden locks and blending with the dazzling sunshine, which painted its reflection on the undulating water. Glittering wings flitted through the young foliage, and the timid lizards darted over the rocks on the shore, which looked as crumbling and moss-grown as if they might tell tales of the days when the castle fountain had stood here in the place of the pool, and from its cool depths rose the nixie to tell the lovely, high-born dame of the marvels never before beheld, in order to draw her down into the waves, leaving the proud halls desolate, until they slowly crumbled, thorns and thistles grew over them, and the spring beneath hollowed its bed among them.

Fleecy clouds drifted across the sky, and a red-and-white streamer fluttered amid the distant tree-tops.

Then the sand on the path creaked, a dry branch in the grass snapped, and Marie, startled, raised her head, then sprang up with a low, exulting cry. He stood before her.

A burning blush flamed in her cheeks; her dark lashes drooped in charming embarrassment; then rose, revealing eyes beaming with delight. She advanced to meet him—then paused timidly. Her rosy lips trembled, but found no fitting words. What was she to say?

Traugott stood smiling down at her, raised his arms, and silently extended them.

The little bird on the bough caroled a joyous love-song, and Marie rushed into the open arms to nestle on her lover's breast.

"Traugott!" she murmured, with an indescribable blending of love and timidity.—"Traugott!"

The sun sparkled on the water; the boughs swayed above their heads; the little songster suddenly spread its wings and soared upward to the blue sky, announcing to the radiant·universe the new yet ever old story of binding and eternal troth.

They sat together on the mossy trunk, unable to find language to utter the feelings of their hearts. Marie leaned her head on the young mill-owner's breast, listening with throbbing pulses to the unfamiliar words of happiness and fidelity.

Suddenly she started up. "Traugott," she asked, a still deeper flush crimsoning her cheeks, "have you opened my memento?"

A line of pain marked the forehead of the handsome officer, gliding like an icy breath over his radiant features.

"Why do you remind me of my talisman now, Marie?" he said, almost reproachfully. "Must its memory embitter even the happiest moment of my life?"

The young girl gazed deep into his eyes; then, with an almost mischievous expression, answered:

"It *is* cruel, isn't it? And yet I must grieve you with it. Where is my amulet, Traugott?"

He silently unfastened his coat, slipped the ribbon from his neck, and gave her the untouched secret.

Marie's face blanched.

"This ribbon"—the words fell from her lips like a cry of fear—"this ribbon is red—the end has drunk your blood!"

She threw her arms around his neck with sudden terror, as if to guard her lover from the murderous bullet.

Then her fingers broke the seal, the covering of his unknown talisman fell, and the slender white hand was held out to him. But no, he was dreaming—it was impossible. He was mad to believe that this was his cross—his locket.

Oh, all was delusion—the girlish figure before him was a vision of his fevered brain, and the whole scene a mere illusion of his crazed fancy! He was still lying in the gloomy hospital. Would he not wake presently, and—but no! The fresh May breeze was blowing through the branches, the sun was laughing in the heavens, and the young girl was Marie, his own beloved Marie, who held in her hand his locket, his cross, which the lake had swallowed before his eyes!

He rubbed his forehead and stared at the miracle in her fingers. He could not believe his eyes.

"Marie!" he cried at last. "Am I awake? Am I out of my senses? Or do miracles happen still?"

Marie laughed joyously, and pressed the treasure into his hand:

"Here, here, take it, dearest! It is your own property, which has so long accompanied you with my love and my blessing. Oh, look at it, Traugott—your locket, your flower, your precious legacy! Surely you recognize it, only you don't understand how it came into my possession, and deem love so weak, so timorous, that it cannot wrest its treasure from the waves. The lake *must* open its icy arms when the voice of the heart commands. The depths must yield their booty when a faithful hand demands it; and now believe the miracle, you doubter, and be happy—happier than you ever were before."

Traugott, deeply agitated, gazed long and earnestly into the beautiful eyes of the woman he loved, covered her little hand with kisses, pressed it with its treasure to his throbbing heart, and again examined the genuineness of the gift, in whose reality he could yet scarcely believe. But here within were the letters of his father's name; here still lay the white flower of death, uninjured! Ay, it was indeed his precious property!

A tumult of bliss took possession of his soul, intoxicating him with its resistless might. All sorrows were forgotten, all darkness merged in dazzling light; and the swift alternation of grief and joy confused him. It was too much happiness all at once! Then, when the tumult had partially subsided, when the young man passionately pleaded for an explanation of the miracle, Marie's sweet voice described that night on the lake, when, with Franz, she had cast the net for happiness and drawn up so magnificent a prize; the unutterable anguish which threatened to overwhelm her, and finally the moment when she again held in her hand the treasure so painfully sought, while Traugott listened as though to an incomprehensible tale.

"What can have become of that ballet-dancer?" asked the young girl, pausing suddenly and looking up at him with almost timid glance. "That woman could not have known a moment's happiness from that hour, or she never loved you!"

"She is dead," replied Gerrald, in a sorrowful tone. "She died at peace and reconciled to God and the world. The butterfly flitted through its bright summer of happiness, and enjoyed its short, bright existence; but could not endure the winter of want and sorrow. She succumbed to the shadow which she herself had cast over her sun."

"Then you saw her again? You talked with her?"

The young officer narrated his meeting with the will-o'-the-wisp that had once more crossed his path, suddenly beaming with a milder radiance, and then vanishing in eternal darkness.

"She remained in the hospital and nursed her former lover," Traugott continued, in a tone of deep feeling. "She never left his couch until he fell asleep, and then she glided up to the other rooms, where she talked and jested with her countrymen as though her gay laughter could belie the pallid cheeks which revealed her suffering. I had forgiven her, and this rendered her calm and almost gentle;

but she rarely came and talked with me. She cared for me while I was asleep, and I felt, as if in a dream, lips pressed to my hand, upon which, when I woke, tears were glittering. Heloise coughed violently, and at times suffered from weakness and weariness; but she never complained. On the contrary, she consoled Maurice with jesting words, and soothed him by the smile on her pale lips. Suddenly typhus fever broke out in the French division, and no entreaty, no representations could dissuade Heloise from carrying refreshments to the sufferers. One day she did not return. She herself was one of the first victims."

"And the French cuirassier?" asked the fair-haired girl, with dim eyes.

"He has returned home and tends her grave in the distant South," replied Traugott, gravely. "The unfortunate man had scarcely been able to believe in the reality of his happiness, when it was once more cruelly torn from him. I do not know whether he can bless the sip from my field-flask which kept him alive."

Marie looked up at him with tearful eyes.

"I have been unable to feel aught save hatred and contempt for that woman, and since that hour on the island in the park I have wished for revenge on her, as if I might thus buy back your happiness, Traugott; but when I learned afterwards how great a loss she had sustained through Brand, how she had been found senseless beside the empty casket which had contained her diamonds, how constantly she was obliged to wander through the world, I could not help pitying her, and shuddered at the wild life which brought naught save storms and which bore so little fruit."

Gerrald silently bowed his head and gazed at the shining dragon-fly which fluttered restlessly over the water, and at last, with weary wings, sank into the depths.

"Marie," he suddenly exclaimed, pressing her hand to his lips, with a loving glance, "forget Heloise. Do not suffer the first shadow to pass over our sunny happiness, or waken by her name memories which should now be forever buried and forgotten. My past life is closed to-day. I am beginning a new and promising course, and when I enter your mother's presence in the king's coat, adorned with the cross I have so lately won, please God, she will not refuse me the hand of her child, in which rests all the happiness and confidence of my future! I shall remain in the army, Marie. I have learned to love my sword, and can no longer part from the color which has protected my treasure in battle and danger. Will you become the wife of a soldier, dearest, who can offer you laurels and an honorable sword, but no coronet?"

Marie held out both her hands with a radiant glance.

"You intend to remain in the army?" she cried, exultingly, in an outburst of delight. "Oh, how pleased mamma will be! Come, Traugott, let us take her this glad news at once." The young girl started up excitedly, and was hurrying through the grass and sedges; but she paused suddenly, asking, almost timidly : " And the mills—what will become of the mills, if their owner is away?"

Traugott smiled.

"Lohfeld will be my manager, and I am sure that the wheels will be guided by a faithful hand. True, it will cost a struggle before the men can get accustomed to the new idea; but no matter! And he too must yield, though it is hard to contend against loyalty and devotion.

"Now come, Marie! Ah, how confident and bold I feel, with your cross and the wonderful flower again on my heart! I could dispute your possession with the whole world, and yet I dread your mother's glance. Does she suspect what is to be asked of her?"

"She knows all," whispered the young baroness, "and awaits your coming to complete my happiness. After the long winter comes the spring, and hearts, too, thaw when love shines faithfully and ardently upon them. You will scarcely recognize my mother, Traugott. She is no longer the unapproachable woman of former days, but my loyal, tender mother, who can understand her child, and who knows herself what love is. A short time ago she told me her own love-history, and I perceived, with tears, that, though her heart had been embittered and hardened by sorrow, it had never ceased to throb lovingly for me. Do not ask too much of her at first, dearest; do not expect her to show you a tenderness which she often still denies me. Be content with her friendship and esteem, and do not forget how hard it is to embrace, as a son, a man whose family has always been the object of hatred. Mamma likes you; your uniform will raise you still more in her eye, and at least relieve her of the terrible thought of being compelled to marry her child to a merchant. The feud between the Gerralds and Von Rotterswyls was too deep and had endured too many years to be so swiftly forgotten. The formality of her manner will also disappear, when she sees how truly I love you, Traugott; and when she has once accepted you as her daughter's husband, it will not be long ere she treasures you in her heart as a son."

They walked along the path bordered with yew, brushing the waving tendrils which grew so luxuriantly over the tall stone statues that they were almost hidden beneath the leafage. Their fixed eyes stared down at the young couple, and the wind rustling the tops of the ancient trees and lightly stirring the dust on the moss-grown heads brought a mysterious whisper:

"Wake, thou pallid woman, who so often sat here weeping! Rise, patient Barbara von Rotterswyl, the hour has come for whose fulfillment thou hast prayed with a breaking heart; the chasm is filled, and to-day a great festival is celebrated in memory of you!"

* * * * * *

Old Gretlis sat at the gable window of the venerable Gerrald house, holding the thread in her cold fingers. Her white head had sunk low on her breast, and her eyes were closed for their last, long sleep. A peaceful dream seemed hovering over her, for her lips smiled—a dream of wedding-bells, which had echoed through the open window, and at whose devout sound she had arranged a little bouquet to carry down to the door.

Then she had welcomed her master's young wife to the home of his ancestors, laid her trembling hands in benediction on the beautiful head, tottered into the spacious hall with him, and looked on with beaming eyes as the young wife decorated old Zacharias's portrait with a bridal wreath, and hung the picture of Baroness Barbara at his side. It was a high festival in the life of the faithful maid-servant.

Then she again sat in the bow-window room, busily turning the wheel, till it suddenly stopped, and the thread broke between her fingers. Old Gretlis's shroud was finished.

The venerable house stood as solitary and silent as a tomb, save that the clock on the wall ticked on till, with dull strokes, it struck twelve; then the hands stopped with a sharp snap, like a cry of pain. Its course, too, was run.

The past had ended, and the Book of Time, in which were recorded all its memories, conflicts, hate and love, had closed.

With the dawn of the young morning, a new day-star rose for the House of Gerrald, pouring its sunny light upon the branches of the family tree, and making them put forth leaves and blossoms, and grow with more vigor than ever before, beneath the animating breath of the spirit of the age. And the good genuises of the ancient race whispered, smiling, in Traugott's ear:

"Hail to you and your House, oh, happy Prince of the Mill!"

THE END.

www.ingramcontent.com/pod-product-compliance
Lightning Source LLC
Chambersburg PA
CBHW031937230426
43672CB00010B/1949